I0020806

OSINT CRACKING TOOLS

MALTEGO, SHODAN, AIRCRACK-NG, RECON-NG

4 BOOKS IN 1

BOOK 1
MASTERING OSINT WITH MALTEGO: CLI COMMANDS FOR BEGINNERS TO EXPERTS

BOOK 2
HARNESSING SHODAN: CLI TECHNIQUES FOR OSINT PROFESSIONALS

BOOK 3
AIRCRAFT-NG UNLEASHED: ADVANCED CLI MASTERY IN OSINT INVESTIGATIONS

BOOK 4
RECON-NG COMMAND LINE ESSENTIALS: FROM NOVICE TO OSINT PRO

ROB BOTWRIGHT

Published by Rob Botwright
Library of Congress Cataloging-in-Publication Data
ISBN 978-1-83938-608-4
Cover design by Rizzo

Disclaimer

The contents of this book are based on extensive research and the best available historical sources. However, the author and publisher make no claims, promises, or guarantees about the accuracy, completeness, or adequacy of the information contained herein. The information in this book is provided on an "as is" basis, and the author and publisher disclaim any and all liability for any errors, omissions, or inaccuracies in the information or for any actions taken in reliance on such information. The opinions and views expressed in this book are those of the author and do not necessarily reflect the official policy or position of any organization or individual mentioned in this book. Any reference to specific people, places, or events is intended only to provide historical context and is not intended to defame or malign any group, individual, or entity. The information in this book is intended for educational and entertainment purposes only. It is not intended to be a substitute for professional advice or judgment. Readers are encouraged to conduct their own research and to seek professional advice where appropriate. Every effort has been made to obtain necessary permissions and acknowledgments for all images and other copyrighted material used in this book. Any errors or omissions in this regard are unintentional, and the author and publisher will correct them in future editions.

BOOK 1 - MASTERING OSINT WITH MALTEGO: CLI COMMANDS FOR BEGINNERS TO EXPERTS

BOOK 2 - HARNESSING SHODAN: CLI TECHNIQUES FOR OSINT PROFESSIONALS

BOOK 3 - AIRCRAFT-NG UNLEASHED: ADVANCED CLI MASTERY IN OSINT INVESTIGATIONS

BOOK 4 - RECON-NG COMMAND LINE ESSENTIALS: FROM NOVICE TO OSINT PRO

Introduction

Welcome to the world of Open Source Intelligence (OSINT), where information is power, and the tools at your disposal can make all the difference. In this comprehensive book bundle, "OSINT Cracking Tools," we embark on a journey through the cutting-edge realm of OSINT using four powerful and indispensable tools: Maltego, Shodan, Aircrack-ng, and Recon-ng.

In an age where digital footprints are ubiquitous, the ability to gather, analyze, and leverage open-source information is a skill that has become increasingly vital. Whether you're a novice just starting your OSINT journey or an experienced professional seeking to refine your techniques, this bundle is designed to cater to a wide range of expertise, from beginners to experts.

"Book 1 - Mastering OSINT with Maltego: CLI Commands for Beginners to Experts" serves as your initiation into the world of OSINT, focusing on the versatile tool Maltego. We guide you through its Command Line Interface (CLI) capabilities, from basic entity transformations to advanced graphing techniques. By the end of this book, you will be equipped with the skills necessary to harness Maltego's power for OSINT investigations of all scales.

"Book 2 - Harnessing Shodan: CLI Techniques for OSINT Professionals" immerses you in the capabilities of Shodan, a search engine for internet-connected devices. Starting with setting up your Shodan CLI environment, you'll learn how to perform basic and advanced searches, monitor devices and services, explore Shodan exploits, and delve into real-world case studies. Your journey with Shodan will empower you to conduct OSINT investigations like a pro.

"Book 3 - Aircrack-ng Unleashed: Advanced CLI Mastery in OSINT Investigations" takes you into the world of wireless security assessments. From capturing and analyzing wireless packets to cracking WEP and WPA/WPA2 encryption, you'll explore advanced Wi-Fi attacks, evading detection, and real-world OSINT investigations. This book equips you with the skills necessary to secure wireless networks and uncover vulnerabilities.

"Book 4 - Recon-ng Command Line Essentials: From Novice to OSINT Pro" introduces you to the versatile Recon-ng, an open-source reconnaissance tool. We guide you through setting up your Recon-ng CLI environment, executing basic reconnaissance commands, and advancing to data gathering and analysis. Automation, scripting, and real-world OSINT investigations elevate your skills as a professional intelligence gatherer.

Whether you're interested in uncovering digital footprints, securing wireless networks, or conducting deep OSINT investigations, this book bundle offers you a comprehensive toolkit. Each tool provides a unique perspective on OSINT, ensuring that you have the expertise needed to tackle a broad spectrum of challenges.

We invite you to explore this book bundle, dive into the world of OSINT, and unlock the potential of these cracking tools. Join us on this educational journey as we equip you with the knowledge and skills to excel in the dynamic and ever-evolving field of Open Source Intelligence. Your adventure begins now.

BOOK 1
MASTERING OSINT WITH MALTEGO
CLI COMMANDS FOR BEGINNERS TO EXPERTS

ROB BOTWRIGHT

Chapter 1: Introduction to OSINT and Maltego

In the realm of open-source intelligence, commonly referred to as OSINT, lies the foundation of modern-day information gathering and analysis, a critical component of various fields, from cybersecurity to law enforcement and beyond. OSINT represents the art and science of extracting valuable, unclassified information from publicly available sources, with the primary goal of assisting decision-makers in making informed choices, mitigating risks, and solving complex problems. The significance of OSINT in today's digital age cannot be overstated, as the internet and the proliferation of data have made it an indispensable tool for individuals, organizations, and governments seeking to uncover hidden insights, track trends, and stay ahead of potential threats.

At its core, OSINT relies on the principle of collecting, analyzing, and interpreting information from a wide array of sources that are openly accessible to anyone with an internet connection. These sources can include websites, social media platforms, news articles, blogs, forums, publicly available databases, government publications, and more. The beauty of OSINT lies in its inclusivity; it encompasses an expansive range of data types, from text and images to videos and metadata, making it a versatile discipline that can be applied across various domains.

To fully grasp the essence of OSINT, it is essential to understand the underlying principles that govern its practice. One such principle is the notion of transparency in data collection, where OSINT practitioners rely on information that is willingly shared or published by individuals, organizations, or entities in the public domain. This means that OSINT does not involve any unauthorized access, hacking, or illegal activities to obtain information. Instead, it adheres to ethical and legal boundaries, respecting privacy and ensuring that the data collected is obtained through legitimate means.

Another fundamental aspect of OSINT is its emphasis on open-source tools and techniques. OSINT professionals employ a variety of tools, both commercial and open-source, to facilitate data collection and analysis. These tools range from web scrapers and search engines to specialized software designed for extracting insights from different data types. The combination of these tools with analytical skills and domain expertise forms the core of OSINT operations, enabling practitioners to piece together the puzzle of information from disparate sources.

In the context of OSINT, one cannot overlook the critical role played by information verification and credibility assessment. As information flows freely on the internet, there is a heightened risk of encountering false, misleading, or manipulated data. OSINT practitioners must employ rigorous methods to assess the reliability and authenticity of the information they gather. This involves cross-referencing data from multiple sources, verifying the credibility of the sources themselves, and applying critical thinking to detect potential biases or inaccuracies.

OSINT also places a strong emphasis on the concept of the "intelligence cycle." This cycle consists of several phases, including planning and direction, collection, processing, analysis, dissemination, and feedback. Each phase is interconnected and iterative, with the goal of continually refining the intelligence-gathering process. OSINT practitioners follow this cycle diligently to ensure that the information collected is not only accurate but also actionable, providing decision-makers with insights that can inform their strategies and decisions.

The application of OSINT extends to a wide range of domains and industries. In the field of cybersecurity, for example, OSINT plays a pivotal role in threat intelligence, helping organizations identify potential vulnerabilities, track cyber threats, and assess their own security posture. Law enforcement agencies leverage OSINT to support investigations, locate missing persons, and monitor criminal activities on the internet. Competitive intelligence professionals use OSINT to gain insights into market trends, competitor strategies, and customer sentiment. Even journalists harness OSINT techniques to fact-check information, uncover stories, and investigate issues of public interest.

To harness the full potential of OSINT, individuals must develop a comprehensive skill set that includes proficiency in data collection, data analysis, and critical thinking. OSINT practitioners need to be adept at using a wide range of tools and techniques, from search engine operators to social media monitoring platforms, and from data visualization software to geospatial analysis tools. They must also possess the ability to synthesize large volumes of information into meaningful, actionable intelligence.

Moreover, ethical considerations are paramount in the practice of OSINT. Practitioners must adhere to a strict code of ethics, respecting privacy rights, avoiding harassment, and refraining from engaging in any activities that may harm individuals or organizations. Transparency and honesty are the cornerstones of responsible OSINT practices, ensuring that the discipline remains a force for good in the modern information landscape.

As we delve deeper into the intricacies of OSINT, this book will provide a comprehensive guide to mastering the tools, techniques, and principles of open-source intelligence. Whether you are a novice looking to build a foundation in OSINT or an experienced practitioner seeking to enhance your skills, the chapters that follow will equip you with the knowledge and insights needed to excel in the world of open-source intelligence. With practical examples, case studies, and expert tips, this book will be your companion on a journey to becoming a proficient OSINT professional, capable of navigating the vast ocean of information available in the digital age and using it to make informed decisions, solve complex problems, and contribute to the greater good.

In the realm of open-source intelligence, Maltego stands as a powerful and versatile tool, serving as a linchpin in the information-gathering process for professionals across various fields. Its significance in the world of OSINT cannot be overstated, given its ability to transform raw data from a multitude of sources into structured, actionable intelligence. Maltego's role extends beyond being just another piece of software; it is an enabler, a force multiplier, and a bridge between the vast sea of information and the insights that decision-makers seek.

At its core, Maltego operates as a visual link analysis tool, allowing users to create, explore, and manipulate data graphs that represent connections, relationships, and patterns within complex datasets. These graphs serve as a canvas on which investigators can map out their OSINT investigations, bringing order to the chaos of information scattered across the internet. Maltego's unique strength lies in its ability to amalgamate diverse data types, from web pages and social media profiles to DNS records and IP addresses, into a cohesive, interconnected network.

Maltego's value proposition is rooted in its adaptability and scalability. Whether you are a beginner taking your first steps in OSINT or an experienced professional conducting large-scale investigations, Maltego can be tailored to meet your specific needs. Its versatility makes it equally suitable for tracking individuals, uncovering organizational structures, or analyzing cyber threats. Maltego's capabilities extend beyond mere data visualization; it empowers users to query, transform, and analyze data in real-time, delivering actionable insights at every stage of an investigation.

One of the defining features of Maltego is its vast ecosystem of transforms. Transforms are plugins that enable Maltego to interact with external data sources and APIs, fetching information and enriching the graph with valuable context. Maltego's ability to seamlessly integrate with these transforms opens up a world of possibilities for OSINT practitioners, granting access to a wealth of data points from sources such as social media platforms, domain registrars, geolocation databases, and more. This capability to pivot between internal and external data sources is what sets Maltego apart as a powerhouse in OSINT.

Beyond its technical capabilities, Maltego fosters a structured approach to OSINT investigations. The process typically begins with defining the scope of the investigation and identifying the key entities and relationships of interest. With this foundation in place, investigators can use Maltego to collect data, analyze patterns, and uncover hidden connections. As the investigation progresses, the data graph grows and evolves, providing a dynamic representation of the evolving understanding of the subject matter.

Maltego's utility extends to a wide range of applications. In the realm of cybersecurity, it plays a crucial role in threat intelligence, aiding organizations in identifying potential vulnerabilities, tracking malicious actors, and assessing their own digital footprint. Law enforcement agencies leverage Maltego to assist in criminal investigations, locate missing persons, and unravel complex networks of suspects. In the corporate world, it aids in due diligence investigations, competitive analysis, and risk assessment. The investigative journalism community relies on Maltego to uncover stories, verify information, and connect the dots in investigative reports.

Throughout the chapters that follow, this book will guide you through the intricate landscape of Maltego, providing insights, tips, and techniques to help you harness its full potential in your OSINT endeavors. Whether you are a beginner seeking to master the fundamentals of Maltego or an experienced user looking to refine your skills, the knowledge imparted here will empower you to navigate the ever-expanding universe of open-source intelligence with confidence and precision.

From the basics of installation and configuration to the intricacies of transform customization and advanced graph manipulation, each chapter will equip you with practical knowledge and real-world examples. Case studies and scenarios will illustrate how Maltego can be applied to various use cases, providing a holistic understanding of its capabilities. Whether you are tracking down cyber threats, conducting due diligence on a business partner, or exploring the digital footprint of an individual, Maltego will become an indispensable tool in your OSINT toolkit.

The journey ahead promises to be rewarding, challenging, and enlightening. The art and science of OSINT are continually evolving, and with Maltego as your ally, you will be well-prepared to navigate the complexities of this ever-changing landscape. As you embark on this exploration of Maltego's role in OSINT, remember that it is not just a software application; it is a gateway to uncovering the truths hidden within the vast sea of digital information, ultimately enabling you to make informed decisions, solve intricate puzzles, and contribute to a safer and more informed world.

Chapter 2: Getting Started with Maltego CLI

Installing and configuring Maltego Command Line Interface (CLI) is the first step toward mastering this powerful tool for open-source intelligence (OSINT) investigations. Maltego CLI is designed to provide users with a versatile and efficient way to harness the capabilities of Maltego in a command-line environment. Whether you are a beginner taking your initial steps in OSINT or an experienced investigator looking to expand your toolkit, understanding the installation and configuration process is essential.

To begin, you will need to obtain the Maltego CLI software, which is available for various operating systems, including Windows, macOS, and Linux. The installation process may vary slightly depending on your operating system, but the fundamental steps remain consistent. The official Paterva website is the primary source for downloading the Maltego CLI installer, ensuring that you have the latest version with the most up-to-date features and security enhancements.

Once you have downloaded the installer for your specific operating system, you can initiate the installation process. In most cases, this involves running the installer executable file and following the on-screen prompts. During the installation, you will have the opportunity to customize certain settings, such as the installation directory and any additional components or modules you wish to include. It is advisable to review and confirm these settings to ensure that they align with your requirements.

After completing the installation, the next crucial step is configuring your Maltego CLI environment. Configuration is essential to tailor the tool to your specific needs and preferences. The primary configuration file for Maltego CLI is known as "config.mtz," which can be found in the installation directory. This file contains various settings and parameters that govern the behavior of the CLI.

To configure Maltego CLI, you can open the "config.mtz" file using a text editor of your choice. Within this file, you will find options to specify your API keys for data source integrations, customize the user interface, and define default settings for various aspects of Maltego CLI's operation. These settings are essential to streamline your workflow and ensure that Maltego CLI behaves according to your requirements.

One crucial configuration aspect is the integration of transforms. Transforms are essential components of Maltego CLI, enabling it to interact with external data sources and APIs to retrieve information during your investigations. To configure transforms, you will need to define API keys or authentication tokens for the specific data sources you intend to use. This process ensures that Maltego CLI can access and retrieve data seamlessly during your investigations.

Additionally, you can configure other aspects of Maltego CLI, such as setting the default working directory, specifying the language and localization preferences, and defining the behavior of various modules and components. The configuration process provides you with the flexibility to adapt Maltego CLI to your unique investigative needs.

In the context of OSINT investigations, efficient and effective configuration is crucial to streamline the data collection and analysis process. By fine-tuning your Maltego CLI environment, you can ensure that you have access to the data sources and transforms necessary for your investigations. Additionally, a well-configured environment minimizes potential obstacles and enhances your overall experience with the tool.

As part of the configuration process, you can also create custom entities and transform sets tailored to your specific investigative requirements. This customization allows you to extend the functionality of Maltego CLI and leverage it for specialized use cases. Whether you are tracking individuals, mapping organizational structures, or investigating digital footprints, custom entities and transforms empower you to work more efficiently and effectively.

In addition to customizing the environment, it is essential to stay informed about updates and improvements to the Maltego CLI software. Paterva regularly releases updates and patches to enhance the tool's functionality, security, and stability. It is advisable to periodically check for updates and apply them to ensure that you are using the latest version of Maltego CLI with access to new features and data sources.

Furthermore, as part of your configuration, consider optimizing your workspace to accommodate the unique demands of your OSINT investigations. This includes organizing your data, creating investigation templates, and establishing a workflow that maximizes your efficiency. An organized and well-configured workspace can significantly impact the quality and speed of your investigative work.

In summary, the installation and configuration of Maltego CLI are fundamental steps in your journey to becoming a proficient OSINT investigator. By obtaining the software, customizing it to your needs, and staying updated with the latest developments, you will be well-equipped to leverage the full potential of Maltego CLI in your open-source intelligence investigations. The following chapters will delve deeper into the practical aspects of using Maltego CLI, providing you with insights, tips, and techniques to master this invaluable tool.

Navigating the Maltego Command Line Interface (CLI) is an essential skill for anyone seeking to harness the power of this versatile tool in open-source intelligence (OSINT) investigations. The CLI provides a streamlined and efficient way to interact with Maltego, allowing users to perform various tasks, from initiating investigations to executing transforms and analyzing results, all through the command line. To become proficient in using the Maltego CLI, it is essential to understand its interface and how to navigate it effectively.

At its core, the Maltego CLI interface is text-based, devoid of the graphical elements that one might find in the Maltego Desktop Client. This streamlined interface provides a lightweight and efficient means of conducting OSINT investigations, making it particularly suitable for users who prefer a command-line environment or need to automate their investigative workflows.

When you open the Maltego CLI, you are presented with a command prompt, typically displaying your current working directory and any relevant system information. The command prompt serves as your gateway to interacting with Maltego CLI, allowing you to issue commands and execute actions to drive your investigations forward.

One of the first commands you will become acquainted with in the Maltego CLI is the "run" command. The "run" command is your entry point to initiating investigations and executing transforms. To use it, you simply type "run" followed by the name of the transform or investigation you wish to launch. This straightforward command structure ensures that you can quickly initiate actions without the need for extensive menus or graphical navigation.

The simplicity of the Maltego CLI interface is one of its strengths. It enables users to focus on their investigative tasks without being encumbered by a complex graphical interface. Additionally, the CLI interface lends itself well to scripting and automation, allowing users to create custom scripts that leverage Maltego's capabilities for batch processing and data analysis.

As you navigate the Maltego CLI, you will encounter a range of commands beyond "run" that facilitate various tasks during your investigations. These commands cover a spectrum of functions, from managing workspaces and entities to configuring the CLI environment and accessing help documentation. Each command serves a specific purpose and contributes to the overall efficiency of your investigative workflow.

One crucial aspect of navigation in the Maltego CLI is understanding the concept of workspaces. Workspaces serve as containers for your investigations, allowing you to organize and manage your data and activities effectively. You can create, switch between, and close workspaces as needed, ensuring that you can keep your investigations separate and organized.

Entities are a central component of OSINT investigations, and Maltego CLI provides commands to manage them efficiently. You can create, view, modify, and delete entities using simple commands, enabling you to build and manipulate the data graph that forms the foundation of your investigations.

In addition to managing entities, you can also employ commands to interact with transforms. Transforms are the heart of Maltego's data gathering and analysis capabilities, allowing you to query external data sources and enrich your data graph with valuable information. The Maltego CLI enables you to list available transforms, run transforms on specific entities, and manage transform results.

Navigating the Maltego CLI interface also involves understanding the concept of configurations. Configurations allow you to customize the behavior of Maltego CLI, from specifying default options for transforms to setting preferences for the user interface. Configurations ensure that the tool aligns with your investigative requirements and streamlines your workflow.

As you become more proficient in using the Maltego CLI, you will find that mastering keyboard shortcuts and command syntax can significantly enhance your productivity. Maltego CLI provides a range of keyboard shortcuts for common actions, such as saving workspaces or executing commands. Additionally, understanding the syntax and parameters of commands will enable you to issue precise instructions to Maltego CLI.

The navigation of the Maltego CLI interface is a skill that improves with practice. As you conduct more investigations and become familiar with the commands and workflows, you will find yourself moving swiftly and confidently through the CLI. The efficiency and versatility of the CLI make it a valuable asset for OSINT professionals seeking to extract insights from data and uncover hidden connections in the digital landscape.

In the following chapters, you will delve deeper into the practical aspects of using the Maltego CLI, exploring real-world examples and scenarios that showcase its capabilities. Whether you are conducting cybersecurity investigations, gathering intelligence for law enforcement, or exploring digital footprints in corporate environments, the knowledge and skills you gain in navigating the Maltego CLI will be a valuable asset in your journey as an OSINT investigator.

Chapter 3: Basic Entity Transformations

Creating and editing entities are fundamental skills in the realm of open-source intelligence (OSINT) investigations, as they form the building blocks of your data graph in Maltego Command Line Interface (CLI). Entities are the representations of objects, individuals, or data points that you manipulate and connect to uncover insights, relationships, and patterns during your investigations. Understanding how to create and edit entities effectively is essential to harnessing the full power of Maltego CLI in your investigative work.

Entities in Maltego CLI come in various types, each designed to represent a specific category of information. These entity types range from individuals and organizations to online accounts, IP addresses, websites, and more. The diverse array of entity types allows you to model a wide range of subjects and data points relevant to your OSINT investigations.

To create an entity in Maltego CLI, you use a straightforward command that specifies the entity type and provides the necessary attributes or properties. These attributes vary depending on the entity type and may include details such as names, addresses, phone numbers, URLs, or any other relevant information. By providing these attributes, you build a comprehensive profile of the subject you are investigating.

Once you have created an entity, it becomes a part of your data graph, visible in the workspace where you are conducting your investigation. The entity is represented as a node in the graph, and its appearance and properties can be customized to enhance your understanding and visualization of the data.

Entities can be edited and modified as needed throughout the course of your investigation. Editing an entity involves updating its attributes or properties to reflect new information or changes. For example, if you are tracking an individual's online presence and discover a new social media profile, you can edit the existing entity to add the new profile URL and relevant details.

Entities can also be connected to one another, forming relationships that represent connections, associations, or interactions between different data points. These relationships are crucial for visualizing and analyzing complex networks of information. By connecting entities, you create a visual representation of the connections between individuals, organizations, websites, and other entities in your investigation.

The process of connecting entities in Maltego CLI is straightforward. You use a command that specifies the source entity, the target entity, and the type of relationship between them. This command establishes a connection between the two entities in your data graph, allowing you to explore the relationships and dependencies between different data points.

Entities in Maltego CLI are not static; they can evolve and change as your investigation progresses. As you gather new information or discover additional data sources, you can update and enrich your entities to reflect the latest insights. This adaptability ensures that your data graph remains current and relevant throughout the course of your investigation.

Furthermore, entities in Maltego CLI can be organized into groups or sets. Grouping entities allows you to categorize and manage them efficiently, particularly in investigations with large volumes of data. For example, you can create a group for individuals, another for organizations, and a third for websites, making it easier to navigate and analyze your data graph.

The ability to customize and categorize entities enhances your ability to explore and visualize data in a way that aligns with your investigative objectives. It allows you to focus on specific aspects of your investigation, whether you are mapping out an individual's online presence, identifying connections between organizations, or tracking the digital footprint of a website.

In addition to creating and editing entities manually, Maltego CLI offers the capability to automate entity creation through the use of custom transforms. Transforms are plugins that enable Maltego CLI to interact with external data sources and APIs to retrieve information automatically. This automation streamlines the process of populating your data graph with entities, particularly when dealing with large-scale investigations or recurring data collection tasks.

As you become proficient in creating and editing entities in Maltego CLI, you will discover that these skills are at the core of your OSINT investigative work. Entities are the tangible representations of the data points you collect and analyze, and your ability to model, connect, and manipulate them directly impacts the depth and accuracy of your insights.

In the following chapters, you will explore practical examples and scenarios that demonstrate the creation and editing of entities in real-world OSINT investigations. Whether you are tracking individuals, mapping out organizational structures, or uncovering hidden connections in the digital landscape, mastering the art of entity management in Maltego CLI will be a valuable asset in your journey as an OSINT investigator.

Running basic transformations is a fundamental aspect of open-source intelligence (OSINT) investigations in Maltego Command Line Interface (CLI), as it enables you to retrieve valuable information from external data sources and enrich your data graph. Transformations in Maltego CLI are plugins that facilitate the interaction between your investigative environment and various online databases, APIs, and web services, allowing you to query and retrieve data automatically. Understanding how to run basic transformations effectively is essential for gathering actionable intelligence and uncovering insights during your investigations.

Transformations in Maltego CLI are organized into categories based on their functionality and purpose. These categories include OSINT, infrastructure, location, person, organization, and more. Each category contains a set of transformations that are designed to retrieve specific types of information related to entities in your data graph.

To run a basic transformation in Maltego CLI, you use a straightforward command structure that specifies the target entity and the desired transformation. For example, if you have an email address entity and want to run a transformation to gather information related to that email address, you would issue a command that identifies the target entity and specifies the transformation to be executed.

Transformations can be customized and configured to suit your specific investigative needs. You can adjust parameters, set options, and define preferences for individual transformations, tailoring them to the requirements of your investigation. This customization ensures that the transformations align with your objectives and help you gather relevant data.

One of the key benefits of running basic transformations in Maltego CLI is the ability to automate data retrieval. Instead of manually searching for information on various websites or databases, transformations allow you to fetch data quickly and efficiently, saving time and effort in your investigative work. This automation is particularly valuable in large-scale or repetitive investigations where data collection is a significant component.

Transformations also enable you to uncover hidden relationships and connections between entities in your data graph. By querying external data sources and retrieving relevant information, you can establish links and dependencies that may not be apparent through manual research alone. These connections provide valuable context and insight into your investigation.

Furthermore, the results of transformations are seamlessly integrated into your data graph, allowing you to visualize and analyze the retrieved information alongside your existing entities. This integration enhances your ability to explore relationships, detect patterns, and draw conclusions based on the combined data from multiple sources.

In addition to running individual transformations, you can also perform batch transformations in Maltego CLI. Batch transformations allow you to execute multiple transformations simultaneously, streamlining the process of collecting data from various sources. This capability is particularly useful when you need to gather data related to multiple entities in your investigation.

To run batch transformations, you specify a list of target entities and the transformations to be applied to each entity. Maltego CLI then processes the transformations in parallel, retrieving data for all specified entities efficiently. This approach is beneficial when dealing with large datasets or conducting investigations that involve multiple entities.

As you become more proficient in running basic transformations, you will discover that the real power of Maltego CLI lies in its ability to adapt to a wide range of investigative scenarios. Whether you are tracking individuals, conducting due diligence on organizations, or exploring digital footprints on the internet, transformations provide you with the agility to gather the information you need quickly and effectively.

It is essential to exercise due diligence and ethical considerations when running transformations in your investigations. Ensure that you have the necessary permissions or rights to access and retrieve data from external sources, and always adhere to the terms of use and legal requirements associated with the data sources you query. Responsible and ethical data collection is crucial to maintaining the integrity of your OSINT investigations.

In summary, running basic transformations is a core skill in Maltego CLI that empowers you to access external data sources, enrich your data graph, and uncover valuable insights during your OSINT investigations. The ability to automate data retrieval, establish connections, and integrate results into your investigation is invaluable in the world of open-source intelligence.

In the following chapters, you will explore practical examples and scenarios that demonstrate the application of basic transformations in real-world OSINT investigations. Whether you are extracting information from social media profiles, retrieving geolocation data, or querying domain registration databases, the knowledge and skills you gain in running transformations will be a valuable asset in your journey as an OSINT investigator.

Chapter 4: Advanced Transformations and Filters

Exploring advanced transformation options is a crucial aspect of open-source intelligence (OSINT) investigations in Maltego Command Line Interface (CLI), as it allows you to harness the full potential of transformations and extract valuable insights from external data sources. While basic transformations provide a solid foundation for data retrieval, advanced transformation options offer additional customization, control, and optimization to enhance your investigative capabilities. Understanding how to leverage these advanced options effectively is essential for conducting in-depth and sophisticated OSINT investigations.

Advanced transformation options in Maltego CLI encompass a range of features and techniques that enable you to tailor transformations to your specific investigative needs. These options are designed to provide flexibility, precision, and efficiency in data retrieval, allowing you to fine-tune your transformations for optimal results.

One of the advanced transformation options in Maltego CLI is the ability to specify input parameters for transformations. Input parameters allow you to pass specific values or variables to a transformation, influencing the scope and nature of the data retrieved. By defining input parameters, you can target your transformations with precision, ensuring that you gather the exact information you need from external data sources.

For example, you can use input parameters to specify a particular keyword, date range, or location when running a transformation. This level of granularity enables you to filter and refine the data retrieved, reducing noise and focusing on the most relevant information for your investigation. Input parameters empower you to tailor your transformations to suit different scenarios and objectives.

Another advanced transformation option is the ability to specify output parameters. Output parameters determine how the results of a transformation are presented and integrated into your data graph. By customizing output parameters, you can control the formatting, structure, and placement of transformation results within your investigation.

Output parameters allow you to define the entity type, labels, and properties of the entities created as a result of a transformation. You can also specify the relationships between the newly created entities and existing entities in your data graph. This level of control ensures that transformation results are seamlessly integrated into your investigation, enhancing your ability to analyze and visualize the data effectively.

Furthermore, advanced transformation options in Maltego CLI include the ability to set timeouts and limits for transformations. Timeouts and limits allow you to manage the duration and resources allocated to each transformation, ensuring that your investigative workflow remains efficient and responsive. By setting timeouts, you can prevent transformations from running indefinitely and consuming excessive resources.

For example, you can specify a timeout for a transformation to ensure that it completes within a reasonable time frame. If a transformation exceeds the defined timeout, Maltego CLI will terminate it, allowing you to proceed with your investigation without unnecessary delays. Timeout settings are particularly valuable when dealing with transformations that may encounter slow or unresponsive external data sources.

Similarly, you can set limits on the number of results retrieved by a transformation. Limiting the results ensures that you obtain a manageable and relevant subset of data, especially when dealing with data sources that may return extensive datasets. By defining result limits, you can focus on the most critical information while avoiding overwhelming your data graph with excessive entities.

Additionally, advanced transformation options include the ability to schedule and automate transformations. Automation is a powerful feature that enables you to execute transformations at specific intervals or trigger them based on predefined conditions. This automation streamlines your investigative workflow, allowing you to continuously monitor and collect data without manual intervention.

Scheduled transformations are particularly valuable for ongoing investigations, where you need to retrieve and update information regularly. For example, you can schedule a transformation to run daily or weekly to track changes in online profiles or monitor updates to domain registration records. Automation ensures that your investigation remains up-to-date and responsive to evolving data.

Another advanced transformation option is the ability to configure error handling and notifications. Error handling options allow you to define how Maltego CLI should respond to errors or exceptions encountered during transformations. You can specify actions such as logging errors, retrying failed transformations, or terminating the entire transformation process.

Notifications enable you to receive alerts and notifications when specific conditions are met during transformations. For example, you can configure notifications to alert you when a transformation encounters a critical error, when a predefined threshold of results is reached, or when specific keywords or patterns are detected in the data. Notifications keep you informed and proactive in managing your investigation.

In summary, exploring advanced transformation options in Maltego CLI empowers you to tailor your transformations to the unique requirements of your open-source intelligence investigations. Input parameters, output parameters, timeouts, limits, automation, error handling, and notifications provide you with the flexibility, precision, and efficiency needed to extract valuable insights from external data sources.

In the following chapters, you will delve deeper into practical examples and scenarios that demonstrate the application of advanced transformation options in real-world OSINT investigations. Whether you are fine-tuning your transformations for specific investigative objectives, automating data collection tasks, or optimizing your workflow for efficiency, the knowledge and skills you gain will be invaluable in your journey as an OSINT investigator.

Filtering and refining search results is a critical aspect of open-source intelligence (OSINT) investigations in Maltego Command Line Interface (CLI), as it allows you to extract actionable insights from the data you have gathered.

While transformations provide a wealth of information, it's essential to apply filters and refine your search results to focus on the most relevant and meaningful data points. This process enhances your ability to analyze and visualize the data effectively, ultimately leading to more informed decisions and insights.

Filtering and refining search results can be approached in various ways, depending on the specific goals and objectives of your investigation. One of the primary techniques is to apply filters based on criteria such as relevance, date, location, or specific attributes of the data. These filters help you narrow down your search results to the data points that are most pertinent to your investigation.

For instance, you can filter search results to include only entities that match specific keywords, ensuring that the data you analyze is directly related to your investigative objectives. This keyword-based filtering technique is particularly valuable when dealing with extensive datasets or when you need to focus on specific topics or individuals.

Date-based filters allow you to refine search results to include information within a specific time frame. This capability is essential when conducting investigations that require historical data or when monitoring changes and updates over time. Date filters enable you to track events, trends, or activities that occurred within a defined period.

Location-based filters are valuable when your investigation involves geographical data. By applying location filters, you can restrict search results to entities associated with a particular geographic region, city, or country. This filtering technique is useful for mapping out local connections, identifying regional trends, or investigating location-specific events.

Attribute-based filters provide even more granularity in refining search results. These filters allow you to specify criteria based on entity attributes such as domain names, IP addresses, email addresses, or phone numbers. Attribute-based filtering ensures that the data you analyze aligns with specific identifiers or characteristics relevant to your investigation.

Another advanced technique for refining search results in Maltego CLI is the use of regular expressions. Regular expressions are powerful pattern-matching tools that enable you to define complex search patterns based on specific text patterns or structures. By using regular expressions, you can extract and filter data that adheres to predefined patterns, enhancing your ability to identify relevant information within unstructured text.

Beyond static filters, you can employ dynamic filters and automation to refine search results in real-time. Dynamic filters are rules or conditions that automatically apply to incoming data, allowing you to categorize, prioritize, or take specific actions based on predefined criteria. Automation enhances your ability to manage and process data efficiently, ensuring that you stay focused on the most critical information.

Another aspect of refining search results is data visualization. Data visualization tools and techniques enable you to represent search results graphically, making it easier to identify patterns, trends, and relationships within the data. Visualization enhances your ability to explore complex datasets, identify outliers, and present findings in a clear and understandable manner.

Moreover, Maltego CLI offers the capability to combine and merge search results from multiple sources or transformations. This consolidation of data allows you to create a more comprehensive view of the subject you are investigating. By merging results, you can uncover connections and relationships that may not be apparent when analyzing individual datasets separately.

Refining search results also involves the process of de-duplication. De-duplication ensures that you eliminate duplicate or redundant data points from your results, preventing the inflation of entity counts and simplifying the analysis. De-duplication is particularly important when working with large datasets or when aggregating data from multiple sources.

In addition to filtering and refining search results, it's essential to apply critical thinking and analysis to the data you have gathered. Interpreting search results requires the ability to discern patterns, identify anomalies, and draw meaningful conclusions from the data. Analysis involves asking questions, making hypotheses, and validating findings to uncover insights and uncover hidden connections.

Furthermore, collaboration and sharing of refined search results are essential in OSINT investigations. Maltego CLI offers features for exporting, sharing, and collaborating on your investigation findings. Whether you are collaborating with team members or sharing insights with stakeholders, the ability to present and communicate your refined search results effectively is crucial.

In summary, filtering and refining search results in Maltego CLI are essential steps in the process of transforming raw data into actionable intelligence. These techniques allow you to focus on the most relevant and meaningful data points, enabling you to analyze, visualize, and draw insights from the information you have gathered.

In the following chapters, you will explore practical examples and scenarios that demonstrate the application of filtering and refining search results in real-world OSINT investigations. Whether you are conducting research on individuals, organizations, or online activities, the knowledge and skills you gain in this process will be a valuable asset in your journey as an OSINT investigator.

Chapter 5: Combining Entities and Graphing Techniques

Building complex graphs is a critical skill in open-source intelligence (OSINT) investigations, as it enables you to create rich and interconnected visual representations of data. Complex graphs allow you to explore relationships, uncover patterns, and gain deeper insights into the subjects of your investigation. In Maltego Command Line Interface (CLI), you have the tools and capabilities to construct intricate data graphs that capture the complexity of your investigative objectives.

The process of building complex graphs in Maltego CLI begins with the integration of various data sources and entities. Entities represent data points, individuals, organizations, websites, and other relevant information that you gather during your investigation. These entities serve as the building blocks of your data graph.

Entities in Maltego CLI can be created manually or retrieved through transformations from external data sources. As you progress in your investigation, you will accumulate a diverse set of entities representing different aspects of your subjects. These entities can include names, email addresses, IP addresses, phone numbers, social media profiles, and more.

Constructing complex graphs involves interconnecting these entities to represent relationships, dependencies, and associations. The connections between entities provide context and meaning to your data graph, allowing you to visualize how different data points are related to one another. These connections are essential for understanding the intricate web of information surrounding your subjects.

Maltego CLI provides several techniques for connecting entities within your data graph. The most straightforward method is to use the "link" command, which establishes a direct relationship between two entities. You specify the source entity, the target entity, and the type of relationship you want to create. This technique is effective for modeling straightforward connections between data points.

However, building complex graphs often requires more advanced techniques for handling multiple entities and relationships. Maltego CLI offers the capability to group entities and create clusters to represent related data points. Clusters allow you to organize and visually separate entities that belong to a specific category or context within your investigation.

For example, if you are investigating an organization, you can create a cluster to group entities related to its employees, another cluster for its partners, and another for its online presence. This hierarchical organization makes it easier to manage and analyze complex graphs with numerous entities.

Another advanced technique for building complex graphs is the use of association entities. Association entities act as intermediary entities that connect multiple other entities. By creating association entities, you can represent complex relationships that involve multiple data points or attributes. This technique is valuable when modeling intricate dependencies or interactions within your data graph.

Moreover, Maltego CLI allows you to create entity sets and assign entities to these sets based on specific criteria or categories. Entity sets serve as logical groupings that help you organize and filter entities within your investigation. This organizational structure simplifies the process of managing and working with complex graphs.

Additionally, you can apply labels, icons, and custom properties to entities and relationships to enhance the visualization of your data graph. These visual cues provide context and highlight important information within the graph. Customizing entity properties and labels allows you to convey additional details and insights to anyone reviewing the graph.

Building complex graphs also involves the use of layout and visualization techniques to optimize the presentation of your data. Maltego CLI offers various layout options, such as radial, hierarchical, and circular layouts, to arrange entities and relationships in a visually appealing and meaningful manner. These layout options help you reduce clutter and improve the readability of your complex graphs.

Moreover, you can adjust the size, color, and style of entities and relationships to convey specific information or emphasize certain data points. The customization of visual elements allows you to draw attention to critical entities, highlight relationships, and differentiate between different types of data within your graph.

Furthermore, complex graphs in Maltego CLI can be exported and shared in various formats, including images, reports, and graphML files. Exported graphs are useful for documentation, collaboration, and presenting findings to stakeholders. The ability to share complex graphs ensures that the insights and discoveries from your investigation can be communicated effectively.

In summary, building complex graphs in Maltego CLI is a fundamental skill that allows you to visualize, analyze, and understand the intricate connections and relationships within your open-source intelligence investigations. The techniques and tools provided by Maltego CLI empower you to construct data graphs that capture the complexity of your investigative objectives and uncover valuable insights.

In the following chapters, you will explore practical examples and scenarios that demonstrate the process of building complex graphs in real-world OSINT investigations. Whether you are mapping out organizational structures, tracking individuals, or analyzing digital footprints, the knowledge and skills you gain in this process will be a valuable asset in your journey as an OSINT investigator.

Visualizing relationships and patterns is a crucial aspect of open-source intelligence (OSINT) investigations, as it allows you to gain insights and make sense of the complex web of data you have gathered. In Maltego Command Line Interface (CLI), you have the tools and capabilities to create visual representations that reveal connections, dependencies, and trends within your investigative subjects. The process of visualizing relationships and patterns enables you to uncover hidden insights, detect anomalies, and make informed decisions based on the data at hand.

At the heart of visualizing relationships and patterns in Maltego CLI is the data graph. The data graph is a visual representation of your investigation, consisting of entities and the connections (edges) between them. Entities represent data points, individuals, organizations, websites, and other relevant information, while the connections between entities represent relationships, associations, or dependencies.

The data graph serves as a canvas where you can explore and interact with your investigative findings. It provides a holistic view of your subjects and their interconnectedness, making it easier to identify patterns and trends that may not be apparent through traditional data analysis methods.

To visualize relationships and patterns effectively, it's essential to understand the layout options available in Maltego CLI. Layout options determine how entities and connections are arranged within the data graph. Maltego CLI offers several layout algorithms, including radial, hierarchical, circular, and organic layouts, each suitable for different visualization needs.

The choice of layout depends on the complexity of your data graph and the specific aspects you want to emphasize. For example, a hierarchical layout may be suitable for displaying organizational structures, while a radial layout can be used to highlight the relationships between a central entity and its connections.

Moreover, data visualization techniques such as clustering and grouping are valuable for visualizing relationships and patterns. Clusters and groups allow you to organize and group related entities within your data graph, making it easier to discern patterns and associations. Clustering is particularly useful when dealing with large datasets or when you want to identify commonalities among entities.

By creating clusters or groups, you can reduce visual clutter and focus on specific aspects of your investigation. For example, you can cluster entities related to individuals, organizations, and online profiles separately, allowing you to explore patterns within each category.

Visualizing relationships and patterns also involves the use of colors, labels, and visual cues to convey information within the data graph. You can customize the appearance of entities and connections to highlight specific attributes or properties. For instance, you can assign different colors to entities based on their type or category, making it easier to distinguish between individuals, organizations, or websites.

Labels and icons can provide additional context within the data graph, helping you understand the significance of entities and relationships at a glance. Visual cues, such as arrows or line styles, can indicate the direction of relationships or the nature of connections, further enhancing your ability to interpret patterns and trends.

Furthermore, visualizing relationships and patterns in Maltego CLI allows you to detect anomalies and outliers within your data graph. Anomalies are data points or connections that deviate from the expected patterns or trends. By examining the data graph closely, you can identify entities or relationships that stand out or do not conform to the established patterns.

Detecting anomalies is essential in OSINT investigations, as it may lead to the discovery of hidden connections or unusual behaviors. Anomalies can be indicative of fraudulent activities, security risks, or areas of interest that warrant further investigation. Visualizing relationships and patterns enables you to spot these anomalies and take appropriate actions.

In addition to visualizing relationships and patterns within the data graph, you can apply filtering and querying techniques to focus on specific aspects of your investigation. Filtering allows you to hide or show entities and connections based on predefined criteria, making it easier to isolate relevant data points.

For example, you can apply a filter to display only entities associated with a particular geographic location or time frame. This targeted filtering helps you zoom in on specific patterns or relationships within your investigation.

Querying the data graph involves using search and exploration techniques to retrieve information and identify patterns. Maltego CLI provides powerful querying capabilities that allow you to search for entities based on keywords, attributes, or criteria. Querying enables you to navigate the data graph and explore connections and relationships interactively.

In summary, visualizing relationships and patterns in Maltego CLI is a fundamental aspect of OSINT investigations that empowers you to uncover insights, detect anomalies, and make informed decisions based on your investigative findings. The ability to create meaningful visual representations of data enhances your analytical capabilities and allows you to explore the complex web of information surrounding your subjects.

In the following chapters, you will explore practical examples and scenarios that demonstrate the process of visualizing relationships and patterns in real-world OSINT investigations. Whether you are mapping out social networks, tracking online activities, or analyzing digital footprints, the knowledge and skills you gain in this process will be a valuable asset in your journey as an OSINT investigator.

Chapter 6: Integrating External Data Sources

Adding external data feeds is a valuable technique in open-source intelligence (OSINT) investigations, as it expands your access to relevant and real-time information. In Maltego Command Line Interface (CLI), you can integrate external data feeds to enrich your investigations and enhance your understanding of the subjects you are researching. The process of adding external data feeds enables you to access a wide range of data sources, including news articles, social media updates, threat intelligence feeds, and more.

External data feeds serve as valuable sources of up-to-date information that can complement your existing investigative data. These feeds provide a continuous stream of relevant data points that can help you stay informed about the latest developments related to your subjects. By adding external data feeds to your investigations, you can ensure that your insights are based on the most current and relevant information available.

One of the primary benefits of adding external data feeds in Maltego CLI is the ability to automate data retrieval. Automation eliminates the need for manual data collection and monitoring, saving you time and effort in your investigative work. Instead of constantly checking websites, news sources, or social media platforms for updates, you can configure external data feeds to fetch new information automatically.

For example, you can set up external data feeds to monitor news articles related to specific keywords or entities in your investigation. Whenever a new article matching your criteria is published, the data feed will retrieve and incorporate it into your data graph. This automation ensures that you are always aware of the latest news and developments concerning your subjects.

Moreover, external data feeds can be customized to target specific data sources or websites relevant to your investigation. Maltego CLI allows you to define the sources you want to monitor and the criteria for retrieving data. This customization ensures that the data you receive aligns with your investigative objectives and the sources you trust.

Adding external data feeds also enables you to apply filters and transformations to the retrieved data. Filters and transformations allow you to refine and categorize the incoming data, making it easier to manage and analyze. For example, you can apply filters to exclude irrelevant articles or social media posts that do not pertain to your investigation.

Furthermore, you can use transformations to extract specific data points or attributes from the incoming data feeds. Transformations allow you to convert unstructured data into structured entities within your data graph. This conversion process enhances your ability to analyze and visualize the data effectively.

In addition to news articles and social media updates, external data feeds can include threat intelligence feeds that provide information on security threats, vulnerabilities, and cyberattacks. Integrating threat intelligence feeds into your investigations allows you to stay vigilant and proactive in monitoring potential risks and security issues.

By adding threat intelligence feeds, you can identify indicators of compromise (IOCs) and security events that may affect your subjects. These IOCs can include malicious IP addresses, domain names, email addresses, and more. By monitoring threat intelligence feeds, you can take preemptive measures to protect your subjects and assess potential security threats.

Furthermore, external data feeds can be integrated into automated alerting and notification systems. Maltego CLI allows you to configure alerts and notifications based on predefined conditions or triggers. For example, you can set up alerts to notify you when specific keywords or patterns appear in news articles or social media posts related to your subjects.

Alerts and notifications keep you informed in real-time and enable you to respond promptly to emerging developments. Whether you are tracking reputation management, monitoring brand mentions, or staying vigilant about security threats, external data feeds and alerting mechanisms enhance your ability to act proactively in your investigations.

Additionally, external data feeds can be leveraged for geospatial analysis and monitoring. Geospatial data feeds provide information about the physical locations and movements of individuals or entities of interest. By adding geospatial data feeds, you can track the movements of your subjects, analyze geographic patterns, and detect anomalies in their behavior.

For example, you can integrate geospatial data feeds to monitor the travel patterns of individuals or track the locations of assets or vehicles associated with your subjects. Geospatial analysis enhances your ability to understand the geographic context of your investigations and identify geographic correlations or trends.

In summary, adding external data feeds in Maltego CLI is a powerful technique that enhances your OSINT investigations by providing access to up-to-date and relevant information. These feeds enable automation, customization, and real-time monitoring, ensuring that your insights are based on the most current data available.

In the following chapters, you will explore practical examples and scenarios that demonstrate the process of adding external data feeds in real-world OSINT investigations. Whether you are monitoring news updates, tracking security threats, or analyzing geospatial data, the knowledge and skills you gain in this process will be a valuable asset in your journey as an OSINT investigator.

Incorporating API data into Maltego is a powerful strategy that expands the scope and capabilities of your open-source intelligence (OSINT) investigations. APIs, or Application Programming Interfaces, serve as gateways to access external data sources, services, and platforms, providing you with a vast array of information to enrich your investigative efforts. In Maltego Command Line Interface (CLI), you can harness the potential of APIs to retrieve real-time data, automate data collection, and enhance your analysis, ultimately leading to more comprehensive and insightful investigations.

The incorporation of API data begins with identifying the relevant APIs that align with your investigative objectives. APIs cover a wide range of domains, including social media platforms, news outlets, financial databases, geospatial services, threat intelligence feeds, and more. By selecting APIs that match your specific needs, you can access data that is highly relevant to your subjects and research.

To incorporate API data into Maltego CLI, you need to establish connections and authenticate with the respective APIs. API providers typically require users to obtain API keys or access tokens, which serve as credentials for accessing the data. Once you have acquired the necessary credentials, you can configure Maltego CLI to connect to the API endpoints and retrieve the desired data.

Maltego CLI offers a flexible and extensible framework for integrating APIs into your investigations. You can create custom transforms that interact with APIs to retrieve data and transform it into entities within your data graph. Transforms are scripts or modules that execute specific actions, such as querying APIs, processing data, and creating entities and relationships within the graph.

By developing custom transforms, you can tailor the integration of API data to your unique investigative requirements. These transforms allow you to specify the parameters, filters, and criteria for fetching data from APIs, ensuring that you gather information that is pertinent to your subjects and research objectives.

Moreover, Maltego CLI supports the integration of third-party Python libraries and modules, enabling you to leverage existing tools and libraries for working with APIs. This extensibility allows you to access a wide range of APIs and services, even if they are not directly supported by Maltego CLI out of the box.

Incorporating API data into Maltego CLI facilitates real-time monitoring and data synchronization. APIs provide access to data sources that are constantly updated, such as social media posts, news articles, or financial market data. By integrating these APIs, you can automate the retrieval of new data and ensure that your investigation remains current and responsive to the latest developments.

For example, you can configure Maltego CLI to fetch social media posts related to your subjects and monitor them for updates in real-time. This dynamic data retrieval enables you to stay informed about the latest online activities and conversations concerning your subjects.

Additionally, incorporating API data allows you to enrich your data graph with contextual information. APIs can provide supplementary data that enhances your understanding of the entities and relationships within your investigation. This contextual data can include metadata, geospatial information, sentiment analysis, or historical records.

For instance, when investigating individuals or organizations, you can use APIs to retrieve data such as employment history, social media profiles, or affiliations. This additional context provides a more comprehensive view of your subjects and their digital footprint, enabling you to draw deeper insights and make informed decisions.

Furthermore, the incorporation of API data into Maltego CLI supports geospatial analysis and mapping. APIs that provide geospatial information, such as geolocation data or mapping services, enable you to visualize the physical locations and movements of entities within your data graph. Geospatial analysis enhances your ability to identify geographic patterns, track movements, and detect anomalies in your investigation.

For example, you can integrate APIs that provide geolocation data to map out the travel routes or geographic correlations of individuals or assets associated with your subjects. This geospatial visualization adds a spatial dimension to your investigation, enabling you to uncover insights that may not be apparent through traditional data analysis.

Incorporating API data into Maltego CLI also supports data normalization and standardization. APIs often retrieve data in various formats and structures. By incorporating APIs, you can standardize and normalize the incoming data, ensuring that it aligns with the entities and attributes within your data graph. This data normalization simplifies the analysis and visualization of the data, making it more consistent and coherent.

In summary, incorporating API data into Maltego CLI is a strategic approach that enhances the depth and breadth of your OSINT investigations. APIs provide access to real-time, relevant, and contextual data, enabling you to stay informed, automate data collection, and enrich your analysis. By harnessing the power of APIs, you can transform your investigative efforts into comprehensive and insightful research.

In the following chapters, you will explore practical examples and scenarios that demonstrate the process of incorporating API data into real-world OSINT investigations. Whether you are monitoring online activities, tracking geospatial movements, or accessing real-time financial data, the knowledge and skills you gain in this process will be a valuable asset in your journey as an OSINT investigator.

Chapter 7: Automation and Scripting with Maltego

Writing custom Maltego scripts is a powerful skill that empowers you to extend the functionality of Maltego Command Line Interface (CLI) to suit your specific open-source intelligence (OSINT) investigation needs. Custom scripts allow you to create custom transforms, entities, and functionalities tailored to your unique investigative objectives. These scripts enable you to automate data retrieval, perform advanced data analysis, and interact with external data sources, making your OSINT investigations more effective and efficient.

The process of writing custom Maltego scripts begins with an understanding of your investigative goals and the specific tasks you want to automate or enhance. Custom scripts can be developed in various programming languages, including Python, Java, and JavaScript, depending on your expertise and preferences.

One of the primary benefits of writing custom Maltego scripts is the ability to create custom transforms. Transforms are scripts or modules that define how data is fetched, processed, and transformed within Maltego CLI. Custom transforms allow you to interact with external data sources, APIs, or databases, retrieving data that is relevant to your subjects and research.

For example, you can write a custom transform that queries a social media API to retrieve the latest posts related to an individual or organization you are investigating. This transform can fetch real-time data, analyze it, and create entities within your data graph, providing you with up-to-date information.

Moreover, custom Maltego scripts enable you to define custom entities that represent specific data points or attributes relevant to your investigation. Entities serve as the building blocks of your data graph, and custom entities allow you to model data that may not be covered by standard Maltego entities.

Custom entities can encapsulate attributes such as geospatial coordinates, cryptocurrency transactions, or threat indicators, providing you with a more comprehensive representation of your investigative subjects. By defining custom entities, you can ensure that your data graph accurately reflects the complexities of your research.

Additionally, custom scripts in Maltego CLI support data enrichment and data fusion. Data enrichment involves enhancing the data within your investigation by augmenting it with additional information from external sources. For instance, you can write a custom script that enriches entities with historical data, sentiment analysis scores, or geolocation data.

Data fusion, on the other hand, involves combining data from multiple sources or transforming data into a unified format for analysis. Custom scripts enable you to merge data from various sources, create composite entities, and generate a holistic view of your investigative subjects. This data fusion process enhances your ability to uncover hidden patterns and insights within your data graph.

Furthermore, custom Maltego scripts support advanced data analysis and manipulation. You can write scripts that perform complex calculations, statistical analysis, or machine learning tasks on the data within your investigation. These scripts enable you to extract meaningful insights, identify trends, and make data-driven decisions.

For example, you can develop a custom script that calculates the social influence scores of individuals in your investigation based on their social media activity. This analysis can help you prioritize and focus on the most influential entities within your data graph.

Custom scripts in Maltego CLI also facilitate interaction with external data sources and APIs. You can create scripts that send requests to APIs, retrieve data, and process responses within the CLI environment. This interaction enables you to access real-time information, monitor updates, and automate data collection from external sources.

Moreover, custom scripts allow you to implement specialized data transformation and normalization techniques. You can write scripts that clean and standardize data, ensuring that it adheres to predefined formats and structures. Data transformation scripts make your analysis more consistent and coherent, simplifying the visualization and interpretation of the data.

Incorporating error handling and exception management into custom scripts is crucial to ensure the robustness and reliability of your investigative workflows. You can implement error handling mechanisms that gracefully handle unexpected situations, such as network issues or API rate limits. Proper error handling ensures that your scripts continue to function smoothly, even in challenging conditions.

Additionally, writing custom Maltego scripts involves testing and validation to verify the correctness and effectiveness of your code. Testing allows you to identify and address any issues or bugs in your scripts before they impact your investigations. Comprehensive testing ensures that your custom scripts operate reliably and produce accurate results.

In summary, writing custom Maltego scripts is a valuable skill that empowers you to tailor Maltego CLI to your specific OSINT investigation needs. Custom scripts enable you to create custom transforms, entities, and functionalities, automate data retrieval, and interact with external data sources. By developing custom scripts, you can enhance the depth and breadth of your investigations, making them more effective and efficient.

In the following chapters, you will explore practical examples and scenarios that demonstrate the process of writing custom Maltego scripts in real-world OSINT investigations. Whether you are automating data collection, performing advanced analysis, or integrating external data sources, the knowledge and skills you gain in this process will be a valuable asset in your journey as an OSINT investigator.

Automating repetitive tasks is a key aspect of optimizing your open-source intelligence (OSINT) investigations, streamlining your workflow, and increasing your efficiency as an OSINT investigator. In Maltego Command Line Interface (CLI), you have the capability to automate a wide range of tasks, saving you valuable time and allowing you to focus on higher-level analysis and decision-making. Automation is particularly valuable when dealing with repetitive and time-consuming actions that can be standardized and scripted.

One of the primary benefits of automating repetitive tasks in Maltego CLI is the reduction of manual effort. Many OSINT investigations involve tasks such as data collection, data enrichment, and data transformation, which can be labor-intensive when performed manually. By automating these tasks, you can eliminate the need for manual data entry and processing, freeing up your time for more strategic activities.

For instance, if you frequently need to retrieve data from online sources, you can write custom scripts that automate the data collection process. These scripts can interact with websites, APIs, or databases to fetch data, process it, and integrate it into your data graph automatically. This automation ensures that your data is up-to-date and reduces the risk of errors associated with manual data entry.

Moreover, automating repetitive tasks in Maltego CLI ensures consistency and accuracy in your investigations. When tasks are automated, they are performed consistently according to predefined rules and criteria. This consistency reduces the likelihood of human errors, ensuring that your data and analysis are reliable and reproducible.

For example, you can create scripts that standardize and normalize data within your data graph. These scripts can enforce data formatting rules, validate attributes, and correct inconsistencies automatically. This standardization process enhances the quality and integrity of your data, making it more reliable for analysis.

Additionally, automation allows you to scale your investigative efforts efficiently. As the volume of data and complexity of investigations increase, manually handling repetitive tasks becomes impractical. Automating these tasks enables you to process large datasets, monitor multiple sources, and analyze extensive networks of entities more effectively.

Automation also supports real-time monitoring and alerting in Maltego CLI. You can configure automated processes that continuously monitor data sources, detect changes or anomalies, and trigger alerts or notifications when specific conditions are met. This real-time monitoring keeps you informed about critical developments and enables you to respond promptly to emerging situations.

For instance, if you are tracking social media mentions of a specific keyword or entity, you can automate the process of monitoring social media platforms for new posts or discussions. When a relevant mention is detected, an automated alert can notify you immediately, allowing you to stay informed about the latest online conversations.

Furthermore, automating repetitive tasks in Maltego CLI supports complex data analysis and transformations. You can develop custom scripts that perform advanced calculations, statistical analyses, or machine learning tasks on the data within your investigation. These automated analyses help you extract meaningful insights, identify trends, and make data-driven decisions.

For example, you can create scripts that calculate sentiment scores for social media posts related to your subjects. These sentiment scores provide insights into the public perception and sentiment surrounding your investigative subjects, allowing you to assess their online reputation more effectively.

Automation also enhances data fusion and integration in Maltego CLI. You can automate the process of aggregating data from multiple sources, combining data points, and generating unified views of your investigative subjects. This data fusion enables you to create a comprehensive and holistic understanding of your subjects.

For instance, you can automate the fusion of data from social media platforms, news articles, and financial databases to create a composite profile of an individual or organization. This composite profile provides a consolidated view of your subjects' digital footprint, affiliations, and online activities.

Moreover, automation facilitates the integration of external data feeds and APIs into your investigations. You can automate the retrieval of data from external sources, such as news outlets, threat intelligence feeds, or geospatial services, and incorporate this data seamlessly into your data graph. This integration ensures that your insights are based on the most current and relevant information available.

For example, you can automate the process of fetching real-time news articles related to your subjects and automatically create entities within your data graph based on the content of these articles. This automation keeps your investigations up-to-date and responsive to the latest developments.

In summary, automating repetitive tasks in Maltego CLI is a valuable strategy that enhances your efficiency, accuracy, and scalability in OSINT investigations. Automation reduces manual effort, ensures consistency, and supports real-time monitoring and analysis. By automating tasks such as data collection, data enrichment, and data transformation, you can streamline your workflow and focus on extracting valuable insights from your investigative data.

In the following chapters, you will explore practical examples and scenarios that demonstrate the process of automating repetitive tasks in real-world OSINT investigations. Whether you are automating data collection, monitoring data sources, or performing complex analyses, the knowledge and skills you gain in this process will be a valuable asset in your journey as an OSINT investigator.

Chapter 8: Maltego for Network Reconnaissance

Scanning and enumerating network assets are essential steps in open-source intelligence (OSINT) investigations, as they enable you to identify and gather information about target networks, devices, and services. In Maltego Command Line Interface (CLI), you have the capability to perform network scanning and enumeration to discover assets and their associated details. These techniques are valuable for mapping the digital footprint of organizations, identifying potential vulnerabilities, and assessing the security posture of target networks.

The process of scanning and enumerating network assets begins with defining your scope and objectives. Before conducting any scans, it is crucial to establish clear goals for your investigation and identify the range of IP addresses, domains, or hostnames you want to target. Proper scoping ensures that you focus your efforts on relevant assets and avoid inadvertently affecting unrelated systems.

One of the primary techniques for scanning network assets in Maltego CLI is the use of specialized transforms and modules. These transforms interact with network scanning tools and services to perform scans on target IP ranges or domains. For example, you can leverage transforms that interface with Nmap, a popular open-source network scanning tool, to conduct port scans and identify open ports and services on target hosts.

Moreover, Maltego CLI allows you to perform DNS (Domain Name System) enumeration to discover subdomains and associated IP addresses. DNS enumeration transforms query DNS records to identify subdomains and their corresponding IP addresses. This technique is valuable for mapping the infrastructure of organizations and identifying potential entry points into their networks.

Furthermore, you can perform WHOIS enumeration to gather information about domain registrants and associated organizations. WHOIS transforms retrieve registration data, contact details, and administrative information related to domain names. This data can provide insights into the ownership and management of target domains, helping you establish connections between organizations and their digital assets.

Scanning and enumerating network assets also involve the use of passive reconnaissance techniques. Passive reconnaissance focuses on gathering information without directly interacting with target systems. Maltego CLI supports passive DNS enumeration and OSINT data collection to obtain information about domain associations, historical records, and online footprints.

For example, passive DNS enumeration transforms retrieve historical DNS data, allowing you to analyze changes in domain configurations and identify historical relationships between domains and IP addresses. This information can help you track the evolution of an organization's online presence.

In addition to transforms and passive reconnaissance, Maltego CLI enables the integration of external data sources and APIs for network asset enumeration. You can incorporate data feeds, threat intelligence sources, and geolocation services to enrich your investigation with contextual information about target assets. These external sources provide data points such as geospatial coordinates, threat indicators, and historical data that enhance your understanding of network assets.

For instance, you can integrate geolocation services to map the physical locations of IP addresses associated with target networks. Geospatial data enrichment transforms provide visual representations of the geographic distribution of network assets, allowing you to identify regional patterns and potential points of interest.

Furthermore, Maltego CLI supports the identification of network vulnerabilities and misconfigurations during the scanning and enumeration process. You can use vulnerability scanning tools and services to assess the security posture of target networks and identify potential weaknesses. Transforms that interface with vulnerability databases and CVE (Common Vulnerabilities and Exposures) repositories can provide insights into known vulnerabilities associated with target assets.

For example, you can conduct vulnerability scans on target IP addresses and use transforms to query CVE databases for information about known vulnerabilities affecting the scanned assets. This analysis helps you prioritize security assessments and identify areas of concern within target networks.

Moreover, scanning and enumerating network assets in Maltego CLI enable you to create visual representations of the discovered assets and their relationships. The data graph serves as a canvas where you can map out the network infrastructure, identify connections between assets, and visualize the digital footprint of organizations. Visualizing network assets enhances your ability to identify patterns, assess network topologies, and detect anomalies.

In summary, scanning and enumerating network assets in Maltego CLI are fundamental techniques for OSINT investigations. These techniques allow you to identify and gather information about target networks, devices, and services, ultimately providing insights into an organization's digital footprint and potential vulnerabilities. Whether you are mapping network infrastructure, assessing security posture, or conducting passive reconnaissance, the knowledge and skills you gain in this process will be valuable assets in your journey as an OSINT investigator.

Identifying vulnerabilities and threats is a critical aspect of open-source intelligence (OSINT) investigations, as it helps you assess the security posture of target entities and understand potential risks. In Maltego Command Line Interface (CLI), you have the capability to identify vulnerabilities and threats associated with organizations, networks, and digital assets. This process is vital for proactive threat intelligence, risk assessment, and security analysis.

The process of identifying vulnerabilities and threats begins with a comprehensive understanding of your investigative scope and objectives. You must define the scope of your assessment, specifying the target entities, systems, or networks you want to analyze. This scoping phase ensures that you focus your efforts on relevant assets and vulnerabilities.

One of the primary techniques for identifying vulnerabilities and threats in Maltego CLI is the use of specialized transforms and modules. These transforms interact with vulnerability databases, threat intelligence feeds, and security assessment tools to retrieve information about known vulnerabilities and potential threats. For example, you can leverage transforms that query the National Vulnerability Database (NVD) to identify known vulnerabilities associated with specific software, systems, or organizations.

Furthermore, Maltego CLI supports the integration of external data sources and threat intelligence feeds for real-time threat detection. You can incorporate threat intelligence feeds that provide information about malicious indicators, vulnerabilities, and cyber threats. These feeds deliver data points such as malicious IP addresses, domain names, malware signatures, and attack patterns.

For example, you can integrate a threat intelligence feed that provides real-time data on emerging cyber threats and known malicious indicators. This integration allows you to detect potential threats and vulnerabilities in your investigation and take proactive measures to mitigate risks.

Additionally, you can perform threat actor profiling and analysis to identify potential threats and their associated tactics, techniques, and procedures (TTPs). Maltego CLI enables you to create threat actor profiles by gathering information from various sources, including OSINT data, incident reports, and threat intelligence feeds. These profiles provide insights into the motivations, capabilities, and targets of threat actors.

For instance, you can use transforms to query OSINT data sources for information about threat actors, such as their affiliations, past activities, and attack patterns. This analysis helps you understand the threat landscape and assess the potential impact of specific threats on your investigative subjects.

Moreover, Maltego CLI supports the identification of vulnerabilities and misconfigurations within target networks and systems. You can conduct vulnerability scanning and assessment to detect weaknesses that may be exploited by threat actors. Transforms that interface with vulnerability scanning tools, such as Nessus or OpenVAS, enable you to assess the security posture of target assets.

For example, you can use vulnerability scanning transforms to scan target IP addresses or domains for known vulnerabilities and misconfigurations. These transforms provide detailed reports on identified vulnerabilities, including their severity, affected systems, and remediation recommendations.

Furthermore, identifying vulnerabilities and threats in Maltego CLI enables you to assess the overall security maturity of organizations and networks. You can conduct security assessments and risk evaluations by combining data from multiple sources, such as vulnerability scans, threat intelligence feeds, and OSINT data.

By aggregating and analyzing this information, you can create security risk profiles that highlight critical vulnerabilities, potential threats, and areas of concern. These profiles assist in prioritizing security measures, making informed decisions, and implementing risk mitigation strategies.

In addition to automated techniques, you can leverage manual analysis and expert judgment to identify vulnerabilities and threats in Maltego CLI. Human expertise plays a crucial role in contextualizing and interpreting OSINT data, identifying emerging threats, and evaluating potential risks. Expert analysis complements automated tools and transforms by providing a nuanced understanding of the security landscape.

For instance, you can rely on subject matter experts or security analysts to assess the impact and likelihood of specific threats, recommend security measures, and validate the findings of automated assessments. Expert input ensures that your investigative conclusions are well-informed and actionable.

In summary, identifying vulnerabilities and threats in Maltego CLI is a vital component of OSINT investigations focused on security analysis and risk assessment. These techniques enable you to assess the security posture of target entities, detect potential vulnerabilities, and stay vigilant about emerging threats. Whether you are analyzing known vulnerabilities, profiling threat actors, or conducting security assessments, the knowledge and skills you gain in this process will be valuable assets in your journey as an OSINT investigator.

Chapter 9: Case Studies and Real-World Applications

Practical OSINT investigations are at the core of open-source intelligence work, allowing investigators to gather, analyze, and interpret publicly available information to uncover valuable insights. These investigations encompass a wide range of scenarios, from due diligence checks and cybersecurity assessments to competitive analysis and threat intelligence. Conducting practical OSINT investigations requires a systematic approach, a diverse set of tools and techniques, and the ability to adapt to ever-evolving online landscapes.

At the heart of any practical OSINT investigation is the identification of objectives and goals. Investigators must define the scope of their inquiry, outline the specific information they aim to obtain, and establish the parameters that guide their research. Clear objectives ensure that investigators stay focused and avoid being overwhelmed by the vast amount of available information.

A fundamental step in practical OSINT investigations involves data collection. Investigators leverage a variety of sources to gather information, including public websites, social media platforms, online forums, news articles, government records, and more. The key is to cast a wide net and gather as much relevant data as possible while respecting legal and ethical boundaries.

Tools play a crucial role in practical OSINT investigations, helping investigators efficiently collect and manage data. Investigators use web scraping tools, search engines, data analysis software, and specialized OSINT tools to streamline their efforts. These tools assist in automating data retrieval, processing large datasets, and identifying patterns and trends.

In addition to automated data collection, manual techniques remain essential in practical OSINT investigations. Investigators often perform manual searches, conduct interviews, and engage in social engineering tactics to obtain information that may not be readily available online. This human-centric approach complements automated methods and adds depth to the investigation.

As information is gathered, it must be validated and verified to ensure accuracy and reliability. Investigative findings are subject to scrutiny, and any inaccuracies can lead to false conclusions. Investigators use multiple sources and cross-reference data points to establish credibility and authenticity.

Another crucial aspect of practical OSINT investigations is the preservation of evidence. Investigators document their findings meticulously, maintaining a chain of custody for digital evidence and ensuring that the data remains admissible in legal proceedings, if necessary. Proper documentation is essential for maintaining the integrity of the investigation.

Analyzing the collected data is a pivotal phase in practical OSINT investigations. Investigators sift through the information, identifying connections, patterns, and anomalies. Data visualization tools can aid in this process by creating charts, graphs, and timelines that make complex data more understandable.

In the context of cybersecurity, practical OSINT investigations focus on identifying vulnerabilities and threats. Cybersecurity professionals use OSINT to discover exposed services, misconfigured systems, and potential entry points for malicious actors. The goal is to preemptively address security issues and bolster an organization's defenses.

Threat intelligence is a critical component of practical OSINT investigations in the cybersecurity realm. Threat analysts monitor online forums, hacker communities, and dark web marketplaces to gather intelligence on emerging threats and hacking techniques. This proactive approach allows organizations to prepare for potential cyberattacks and vulnerabilities.

Practical OSINT investigations also play a pivotal role in due diligence processes. Organizations use OSINT to assess potential business partners, merger and acquisition targets, and third-party vendors. By conducting thorough OSINT investigations, organizations can uncover hidden risks, reputational issues, or legal liabilities that may impact their decision-making.

Competitive analysis is another application of practical OSINT investigations. Companies research their competitors to gain insights into market strategies, product offerings, and customer sentiment. This information helps businesses refine their own strategies and stay competitive in the marketplace.

In the realm of law enforcement and public safety, practical OSINT investigations aid in criminal investigations, missing persons cases, and threat assessments. Investigators leverage social media, public records, and online communications to gather evidence and track down individuals or assess potential threats.

Moreover, practical OSINT investigations are increasingly relevant in the context of digital marketing and brand management. Companies use OSINT to monitor online discussions, sentiment analysis, and customer feedback to enhance their marketing strategies and brand reputation.

The ethical considerations surrounding practical OSINT investigations are paramount. Investigators must adhere to legal and ethical guidelines, respect privacy rights, and obtain information through lawful means. Transparency and respect for individuals' privacy are core principles that guide ethical OSINT practices.

In summary, practical OSINT investigations are a versatile and essential tool in various domains, from cybersecurity and business due diligence to competitive analysis and law enforcement. By following a systematic approach, leveraging a diverse set of tools and techniques, and adhering to ethical principles, investigators can harness the power of publicly available information to uncover valuable insights and make informed decisions. Whether you are a cybersecurity professional, a business analyst, or a law enforcement officer, the skills and methodologies of practical OSINT investigations are invaluable in today's digital age.

Analyzing OSINT success stories provides invaluable insights into the practical application of open-source intelligence and its impact on various domains. These real-world examples showcase how OSINT techniques and methodologies have been instrumental in achieving objectives, solving complex problems, and enhancing decision-making processes.

One prominent OSINT success story is related to law enforcement and criminal investigations. In numerous cases, OSINT has played a pivotal role in locating missing persons, apprehending fugitives, and solving cold cases. Investigators leverage publicly available information, including social media profiles, online communications, and public records, to gather clues and leads that were previously inaccessible.

For instance, the use of OSINT in missing persons cases has led to the discovery of crucial information that helped reunite families with their loved ones. By analyzing social media activity, tracking digital footprints, and cross-referencing data points, investigators have been able to narrow down search areas and locate missing individuals.

OSINT has also been a game-changer in the realm of competitive intelligence and corporate espionage prevention. Companies utilize OSINT techniques to monitor their competitors, track market trends, and gather intelligence on industry developments. By analyzing competitor strategies, product launches, and customer sentiment, organizations can adjust their own tactics to gain a competitive edge.

One notable success story involves a technology company that used OSINT to uncover a competitor's upcoming product launch. By monitoring online forums, social media discussions, and patent filings, the company gained early insights into the competitor's plans. This allowed them to adjust their marketing strategy and product offerings in advance, ultimately maintaining a strong market position.

In the field of cybersecurity, OSINT has proven to be an invaluable tool for threat intelligence and vulnerability assessment. Security professionals analyze OSINT data to identify exposed services, misconfigured systems, and potential security weaknesses. By proactively addressing vulnerabilities, organizations can enhance their cybersecurity posture and reduce the risk of data breaches and cyberattacks.

A noteworthy OSINT success story in cybersecurity involves a financial institution that used OSINT to uncover a vulnerability in its web application. By monitoring hacker forums and dark web marketplaces, the institution's security team discovered discussions about a known vulnerability in the software they were using. This early detection allowed them to apply patches and implement security measures before any exploitation occurred, safeguarding customer data.

OSINT has also proven to be a valuable asset in the realm of threat detection and prevention. Threat analysts leverage OSINT data to monitor online discussions, hacker chatter, and threat actor profiles. By staying informed about emerging threats and attack techniques, organizations can proactively defend against cyberattacks and mitigate risks.

In one particular success story, an organization's threat intelligence team used OSINT to identify a new type of phishing campaign targeting employees. By analyzing phishing emails, tracking domain registrations, and monitoring social engineering tactics, the team uncovered a sophisticated threat actor group. This discovery allowed them to implement stronger email filtering and user awareness training to prevent successful phishing attacks.

Moreover, OSINT has been instrumental in due diligence processes for mergers and acquisitions. Companies use OSINT to assess potential risks associated with business partners, acquisition targets, and third-party vendors. By conducting comprehensive OSINT investigations, organizations can uncover hidden liabilities, legal issues, or reputational concerns that may impact their strategic decisions.

A notable success story in due diligence involves a multinational corporation that used OSINT to evaluate a potential acquisition target. By analyzing online news articles, regulatory filings, and social media profiles, they discovered undisclosed legal disputes and financial challenges facing the target company. This information prompted the corporation to reevaluate the acquisition and negotiate more favorable terms.

OSINT success stories are not limited to corporate and law enforcement domains; they also extend to humanitarian efforts and disaster response. Humanitarian organizations leverage OSINT to assess the impact of natural disasters, monitor crisis situations, and coordinate relief efforts. By analyzing satellite imagery, social media data, and real-time reports, these organizations can allocate resources effectively and respond promptly to emergencies.

In a notable OSINT success story related to disaster response, a humanitarian organization used OSINT data to assess the extent of damage caused by a major earthquake. By analyzing satellite imagery and social media posts from affected areas, they were able to identify areas in urgent need of assistance and deploy rescue teams accordingly. This timely response saved lives and provided critical support to affected communities.

Furthermore, OSINT success stories underscore the importance of ethical considerations and responsible data handling. As OSINT practitioners gather and analyze publicly available information, they must always respect privacy rights, adhere to legal regulations, and ensure that data is obtained through lawful means. Transparency and ethical conduct are essential principles that guide the responsible use of OSINT.

In summary, analyzing OSINT success stories highlights the diverse applications and significant impact of open-source intelligence in various domains. Whether in law enforcement, cybersecurity, competitive intelligence, due diligence, threat detection, or humanitarian efforts, OSINT techniques and methodologies continue to provide valuable insights, enhance decision-making, and contribute to the achievement of objectives. By learning from these success stories, practitioners can refine their OSINT skills and contribute to the responsible and effective use of open-source intelligence in today's complex and interconnected world.

Chapter 10: Becoming an Expert: Tips and Tricks for Mastery

Mastering Maltego's advanced features is a significant step in becoming proficient in open-source intelligence (OSINT) investigations. While Maltego's core functionalities provide a strong foundation, its advanced capabilities offer more extensive analytical power and flexibility. These features enable investigators to conduct complex investigations, visualize intricate relationships, and extract valuable insights from diverse data sources.

One of the advanced features in Maltego is the ability to create custom entities and transforms. Custom entities allow investigators to represent specific data types or objects that are not covered by Maltego's default entities. By defining custom entities, investigators can tailor Maltego to their unique needs and extend its capabilities to handle specialized data.

For instance, investigators may create custom entities to represent proprietary data formats, internal records, or industry-specific identifiers. These custom entities can be linked to existing entities in the data graph, facilitating comprehensive analysis.

Moreover, creating custom transforms empowers investigators to access and manipulate data from external sources that are not supported out of the box. Custom transforms serve as connectors between Maltego and external APIs, databases, or web services. They enable the retrieval of real-time data and the execution of advanced queries.

Custom transforms can be particularly useful when integrating with proprietary data sources, industry-specific databases, or custom intelligence feeds. By developing custom transforms, investigators can automate the collection of relevant data and seamlessly incorporate it into their investigations.

Another advanced feature is the capability to script and automate tasks using Maltego's scripting language. Maltego's scripting language allows investigators to create custom scripts that perform complex data manipulation, analysis, and visualization operations. These scripts can be tailored to specific investigative scenarios and data processing requirements.

For example, investigators can write scripts to automate data enrichment, entity classification, or pattern recognition tasks. These automated scripts expedite the analysis process and ensure consistent and standardized data handling.

Furthermore, Maltego's integration with external Python scripts and libraries extends its analytical power. Investigators can execute Python scripts directly within Maltego, leveraging the extensive ecosystem of Python libraries for advanced data analysis, machine learning, and statistical modeling.

The ability to integrate Python scripts enables investigators to harness the full potential of machine learning algorithms, natural language processing, and advanced analytics in their OSINT investigations. This integration supports predictive modeling, sentiment analysis, and data-driven decision-making.

In addition to advanced scripting capabilities, Maltego offers features for fine-tuning and customizing data transformations. Investigators can define custom filters, conditions, and data mapping rules to tailor the transformation of data within the data graph. These customizations enhance the precision and relevance of analytical results.

For example, investigators can set up filters to exclude irrelevant data points, define conditional rules for data categorization, and map attributes to specific entity types. These customization options help investigators refine their analyses and focus on extracting meaningful insights.

Furthermore, Maltego's advanced graph layout algorithms enhance data visualization and exploration. Investigators can choose from various layout options to arrange entities and links in the data graph dynamically. These layouts include radial, hierarchical, and force-directed arrangements, among others.

The choice of a suitable graph layout depends on the complexity of the investigation and the desired visual representation. Investigators can experiment with different layouts to uncover hidden patterns, connections, and anomalies within the data.

Another advanced feature in Maltego is the capability to perform link analysis and social network analysis (SNA). Investigators can use Maltego to analyze relationships between entities, identify influencers, and visualize network structures. This is particularly valuable in OSINT investigations involving social media, organizational hierarchies, or affiliations.

For instance, investigators can analyze social media data to map out connections between individuals, identify key players, and assess the influence of specific accounts or groups. This analysis can be instrumental in understanding online communities, tracking the spread of information, and uncovering hidden networks.

Moreover, Maltego's advanced reporting and documentation features assist investigators in presenting their findings effectively. Investigators can generate customizable reports that include visualizations, entity summaries, and investigative narratives. These reports are valuable for communicating insights to stakeholders, clients, or colleagues.

The ability to customize reports allows investigators to tailor the presentation of findings to the specific needs and preferences of their audience. Whether preparing reports for legal proceedings, business assessments, or threat intelligence sharing, Maltego's reporting features streamline the documentation process.

In summary, mastering Maltego's advanced features elevates the capabilities of investigators in the field of open-source intelligence. Custom entities, transforms, and scripting empower investigators to handle diverse data sources and automate tasks. Fine-tuning data transformations, leveraging graph layout algorithms, and performing link analysis enhance data visualization and analysis. Additionally, Maltego's reporting and documentation features facilitate effective communication of investigative findings. By harnessing these advanced features, investigators can conduct more comprehensive and insightful OSINT investigations, adapting to the evolving challenges of the digital landscape.

Staying updated and evolving as an open-source intelligence (OSINT) professional is essential in a rapidly changing digital landscape. The field of OSINT continually evolves due to technological advancements, new data sources, and emerging threats. As an OSINT professional, it is crucial to adopt a proactive approach to learning and adaptability to remain effective and relevant in your investigative endeavors.

One of the fundamental aspects of staying updated is continuous learning. OSINT professionals must commit to ongoing education and skill development to keep up with the latest trends, tools, and techniques in the field. This dedication to learning ensures that your OSINT skills remain sharp and up to date.

There are various avenues for continuous learning in OSINT. One of the most accessible sources of knowledge is online communities and forums dedicated to OSINT. These communities provide a platform for professionals to share insights, discuss challenges, and exchange information about new developments in the field.

Engaging with fellow OSINT practitioners in online forums allows you to tap into a collective knowledge base and benefit from the experiences of others. These interactions can lead to valuable discoveries, new methodologies, and innovative approaches to OSINT investigations.

Moreover, attending OSINT conferences and workshops is an excellent way to stay updated on the latest industry trends and network with peers. Conferences often feature expert speakers, hands-on training sessions, and discussions on cutting-edge OSINT tools and methodologies. These events offer opportunities to gain firsthand knowledge and exchange ideas with experts in the field.

Additionally, OSINT professionals can benefit from enrolling in formal training programs and courses. Many organizations and educational institutions offer OSINT training programs that cover a wide range of topics, from basic techniques to advanced skills. These courses provide structured learning experiences and often include hands-on exercises and certifications.

Another essential aspect of staying updated is staying informed about legal and ethical considerations in OSINT. The legal landscape surrounding OSINT can vary by jurisdiction and may change over time. OSINT professionals must have a solid understanding of privacy laws, data protection regulations, and ethical guidelines.

Regularly reviewing and staying current with legal and ethical frameworks ensures that OSINT professionals conduct their investigations within legal boundaries and adhere to ethical principles. Compliance with laws and regulations is crucial to maintaining the integrity of OSINT practices and avoiding potential legal liabilities.

Furthermore, OSINT professionals should pay attention to emerging technologies and data sources that can enhance their investigative capabilities. The digital landscape is constantly evolving, with new platforms, data formats, and communication channels emerging regularly.

Being proactive in exploring and experimenting with these technologies allows OSINT professionals to harness their full potential. For example, keeping an eye on emerging social media platforms, instant messaging apps, and data sharing trends ensures that you can adapt your investigative methods to capture relevant data from these sources.

Additionally, staying updated on developments in the field of cybersecurity is essential for OSINT professionals. As cybersecurity threats and attack techniques evolve, OSINT professionals must understand the changing landscape to assess vulnerabilities, identify potential threats, and contribute to threat intelligence efforts.

Cybersecurity training and certifications can provide valuable insights into the evolving threat landscape and equip OSINT professionals with the knowledge to address cyber threats effectively. Understanding cybersecurity principles also enables OSINT professionals to better protect their own digital footprint and sensitive information.

Maintaining a curious and inquisitive mindset is a hallmark of successful OSINT professionals. Curiosity drives the desire to explore new data sources, test innovative tools, and seek out unconventional approaches to investigations. This curiosity often leads to breakthroughs in OSINT research and the discovery of valuable insights.

Furthermore, collaborating with experts from diverse fields can be instrumental in staying updated and evolving as an OSINT professional. OSINT investigations often require interdisciplinary knowledge, and working with subject matter experts in areas such as cybersecurity, linguistics, data analysis, or geopolitics can provide fresh perspectives and enhance the depth of analysis.

Building a network of trusted contacts and partners in various domains allows OSINT professionals to tap into a wide range of expertise and resources. Collaborative efforts can lead to more comprehensive investigations and a deeper understanding of complex issues.

In summary, staying updated and evolving as an OSINT professional is a continuous journey of learning, adaptation, and exploration. OSINT professionals must commit to ongoing education, engage with online communities, attend conferences, and seek formal training to remain at the forefront of the field. Staying informed about legal and ethical considerations, monitoring emerging technologies, and understanding cybersecurity trends are also essential components of professional development. A curious mindset and collaborative approach further enhance an OSINT professional's ability to navigate the evolving digital landscape and uncover valuable insights in an ever-changing world.

Exploring open-source intelligence (OSINT) is a journey into the realm of information gathering and analysis, leveraging publicly available data to uncover valuable insights. OSINT is a discipline that transcends traditional boundaries, encompassing a wide array of sources, techniques, and applications. At its core, OSINT is about harnessing the power of open data to enhance decision-making, solve problems, and address a multitude of challenges across various domains.

The foundation of OSINT lies in the recognition that an abundance of information is accessible to anyone with an internet connection. This information includes data from websites, social media platforms, public records, news sources, and much more. OSINT professionals tap into this vast repository of open data to extract knowledge that can be used for diverse purposes.

In essence, OSINT serves as a digital detective, allowing individuals and organizations to piece together puzzles, gain competitive advantages, mitigate risks, and make informed choices. The applications of OSINT are boundless, ranging from cybersecurity and law enforcement to business intelligence, competitive analysis, and humanitarian efforts.

One of the key principles of OSINT is the concept of "open" information. OSINT relies on data that is publicly accessible and does not involve hacking, intrusion, or illegal activities. It adheres to ethical standards and respects privacy rights, ensuring that investigations are conducted within legal boundaries.

OSINT professionals are adept at navigating the online landscape, using specialized tools and techniques to extract, filter, and analyze data from a multitude of sources. They employ web scraping, data mining, advanced search operators, and data visualization tools to make sense of the digital haystack and locate the proverbial needles of information.

In the realm of cybersecurity, OSINT plays a crucial role in threat intelligence. Security experts utilize OSINT to monitor online forums, hacker communities, and dark web marketplaces, seeking early indicators of cyber threats and vulnerabilities. By analyzing these sources, they can proactively defend against cyberattacks and safeguard digital assets.

Moreover, OSINT is a valuable resource for organizations conducting due diligence checks. Before entering into partnerships, mergers, or acquisitions, businesses use OSINT to assess potential risks and uncover hidden liabilities. OSINT investigations can reveal information about a company's financial health, legal disputes, or reputational issues that may influence strategic decisions.

Law enforcement agencies leverage OSINT to aid in criminal investigations. OSINT data, including social media posts, online communications, and public records, can provide leads, identify suspects, and gather evidence. OSINT complements traditional investigative techniques, enhancing the ability to solve crimes and locate missing persons.

In the world of competitive intelligence, OSINT allows companies to gain insights into their competitors' strategies, market positioning, and customer sentiment. By monitoring online discussions, tracking news articles, and analyzing public data, businesses can make informed decisions and stay ahead of the competition.

OSINT also extends its reach to humanitarian efforts and disaster response. Humanitarian organizations use OSINT to assess the impact of natural disasters, monitor crisis situations, and coordinate relief efforts. By analyzing satellite imagery, social media data, and real-time reports, these organizations can allocate resources effectively and respond promptly to emergencies.

The essence of OSINT is adaptability. OSINT professionals must adapt to the evolving digital landscape, where new data sources and technologies constantly emerge. The field requires a commitment to continuous learning, as staying updated on the latest tools, techniques, and legal considerations is crucial.

The value of OSINT lies not only in the data itself but also in the ability to connect the dots and uncover hidden patterns. OSINT analysts are skilled at identifying relationships between disparate pieces of information, revealing connections that may not be apparent at first glance. This ability to synthesize data and draw meaningful conclusions is a hallmark of OSINT expertise.

Furthermore, OSINT is a multidisciplinary field that benefits from expertise in various domains. OSINT professionals often possess knowledge in areas such as cybersecurity, data analysis, linguistics, psychology, and geopolitics. This interdisciplinary approach allows them to contextualize information and gain deeper insights into complex issues.

The ethical considerations surrounding OSINT are paramount. OSINT professionals must operate within legal boundaries, respect privacy rights, and adhere to ethical guidelines. Transparency and responsible data handling are fundamental principles that guide ethical OSINT practices.

In summary, exploring open-source intelligence (OSINT) is a journey into the world of information discovery, analysis, and application. OSINT leverages publicly available data from a myriad of sources to uncover valuable insights that have a profound impact on decision-making, problem-solving, and addressing challenges across diverse domains. OSINT professionals, guided by ethical principles, play a vital role in harnessing the power of open data to navigate the complexities of the digital age.

BOOK 2
HARNESSING SHODAN
CLI TECHNIQUES FOR OSINT PROFESSIONALS

ROB BOTWRIGHT

Chapter 1: Introduction to SHODAN and OSINT

Exploring Open Source Intelligence (OSINT) is an exciting journey into the world of information discovery, analysis, and application. OSINT is a multifaceted discipline that harnesses the power of publicly available data to uncover valuable insights, solve complex problems, and make informed decisions across various domains. At its core, OSINT is about leveraging open data sources to enhance understanding and address a wide range of challenges in our digital age.

The foundation of OSINT lies in the recognition that a wealth of information is readily accessible to anyone with an internet connection. This information spans websites, social media platforms, public records, news sources, and more. OSINT professionals, whether they are investigators, analysts, or researchers, utilize this extensive repository of open data to extract knowledge that can be applied in diverse contexts.

OSINT serves as a digital detective, allowing individuals and organizations to piece together puzzles, gain competitive advantages, mitigate risks, and navigate the complexities of our interconnected world. Its applications are far-reaching, spanning fields such as cybersecurity, law enforcement, business intelligence, competitive analysis, and humanitarian efforts.

A fundamental principle of OSINT is its reliance on "open" information, which entails using data that is publicly accessible and does not involve hacking, intrusion, or illegal activities. This ethical approach ensures that OSINT investigations are conducted within legal boundaries, respecting privacy rights and adhering to ethical guidelines.

OSINT practitioners possess a unique skill set that equips them to navigate the vast online landscape. They employ specialized tools and techniques to extract, filter, and analyze data from a multitude of sources. These techniques encompass web scraping, data mining, advanced search operators, and data visualization tools, all of which facilitate the process of locating valuable information.

In the realm of cybersecurity, OSINT plays a pivotal role in threat intelligence. Cybersecurity experts rely on OSINT to monitor online forums, hacker communities, and dark web marketplaces, seeking early indicators of cyber threats and vulnerabilities. By analyzing these sources, they can proactively defend against cyberattacks and safeguard digital assets.

Moreover, OSINT is a powerful tool in the due diligence process for businesses. Before entering into partnerships, mergers, or acquisitions, organizations use OSINT to assess potential risks and uncover hidden liabilities. OSINT investigations can reveal information about a company's financial health, legal disputes, or reputational issues, influencing strategic decisions.

Law enforcement agencies leverage OSINT to aid in criminal investigations. OSINT data, including social media posts, online communications, and public records, can provide leads, identify suspects, and gather evidence. OSINT complements traditional investigative techniques, enhancing the ability to solve crimes and locate missing persons.

In the realm of competitive intelligence, OSINT allows companies to gain insights into their competitors' strategies, market positioning, and customer sentiment. By monitoring online discussions, tracking news articles, and analyzing public data, businesses can make informed decisions and stay ahead of the competition.

OSINT also extends its reach to humanitarian efforts and disaster response. Humanitarian organizations use OSINT to assess the impact of natural disasters, monitor crisis situations, and coordinate relief efforts. By analyzing satellite imagery, social media data, and real-time reports, these organizations can allocate resources effectively and respond promptly to emergencies.

The essence of OSINT is adaptability. OSINT professionals must stay attuned to the evolving digital landscape, where new data sources and technologies constantly emerge. The field requires a commitment to continuous learning, as staying updated on the latest tools, techniques, and legal considerations is crucial.

The value of OSINT lies not only in the data itself but also in the ability to connect the dots and uncover hidden patterns. OSINT analysts are skilled at identifying relationships between disparate pieces of information, revealing connections that may not be apparent at first glance. This ability to synthesize data and draw meaningful conclusions is a hallmark of OSINT expertise.

Furthermore, OSINT is a multidisciplinary field that benefits from expertise in various domains. OSINT professionals often possess knowledge in areas such as cybersecurity, data analysis, linguistics, psychology, and geopolitics. This interdisciplinary approach allows them to contextualize information and gain deeper insights into complex issues.

The ethical considerations surrounding OSINT are paramount. OSINT professionals must operate within legal boundaries, respect privacy rights, and adhere to ethical guidelines. Transparency and responsible data handling are fundamental principles that guide ethical OSINT practices.

In summary, exploring Open Source Intelligence (OSINT) is a journey into the world of information discovery, analysis, and application. OSINT leverages publicly available data from a myriad of sources to uncover valuable insights that have a profound impact on decision-making, problem-solving, and addressing challenges across diverse domains. OSINT professionals, guided by ethical principles, play a vital role in harnessing the power of open data to navigate the complexities of the digital age.

Understanding SHODAN's role in OSINT investigations is essential for harnessing the full power of this specialized search engine. SHODAN, often referred to as the "Google for hackers," is a unique tool that focuses on scanning and indexing internet-connected devices and services. Its primary purpose is to provide users with detailed information about the devices, systems, and services exposed to the internet, making it a valuable resource for a wide range of OSINT investigations.

One of SHODAN's core functionalities is its ability to scan the internet for open ports, banners, and service banners. When a device is connected to the internet, it typically communicates through specific ports, each associated with a particular service or application. SHODAN's scans identify these open ports and gather data about the services running on them, such as the service banner, version information, and other relevant details.

This information is invaluable for OSINT practitioners, as it provides insights into the technology stack and configurations of internet-connected devices. For example, SHODAN can reveal the presence of web servers, databases, remote desktop services, and more, along with version numbers and potential vulnerabilities.

SHODAN's search capabilities are a cornerstone of its functionality. Users can perform searches using various filters, search operators, and keywords to pinpoint specific devices, services, or vulnerabilities. This search flexibility allows OSINT investigators to narrow down their focus, extract relevant data, and identify potential targets for further analysis.

One of the distinctive features of SHODAN is its ability to filter search results based on geolocation data. Users can specify geographic regions, countries, or cities to refine their searches. This geolocation filtering is particularly useful for OSINT investigations with a geographical focus, such as tracking the distribution of specific devices or identifying vulnerable systems in a specific location.

Furthermore, SHODAN provides historical data and version tracking, enabling users to assess how internet-connected devices have changed over time. This historical perspective is valuable for tracking the evolution of technologies, identifying when specific vulnerabilities were introduced or patched, and monitoring changes in device configurations.

SHODAN also offers a comprehensive API that allows for programmable access to its data. OSINT professionals can use the API to automate searches, collect data at scale, and integrate SHODAN's functionality into their own tools and workflows. This level of automation enhances the efficiency of OSINT investigations and enables the continuous monitoring of internet-connected assets.

Another critical aspect of SHODAN is its ability to detect and report vulnerabilities associated with internet-connected devices and services. It provides a Vulnerabilities tab for each device in its search results, listing known vulnerabilities based on the service banners and version information collected during scans. This feature is invaluable for identifying potential security risks and prioritizing remediation efforts.

In addition to its scanning and search capabilities, SHODAN offers a paid subscription service called SHODAN Pro. SHODAN Pro provides enhanced access to SHODAN's data, additional search filters, and more advanced query options. OSINT investigators who require deeper insights and broader search capabilities may find SHODAN Pro to be a valuable investment.

Understanding the ethical considerations when using SHODAN is crucial for responsible OSINT investigations. While SHODAN provides access to publicly available information, using it for malicious purposes or attempting unauthorized access to devices or systems is strictly unethical and illegal. OSINT professionals must always operate within legal boundaries and adhere to ethical guidelines when using SHODAN or any other OSINT tool.

Moreover, it's essential to consider the potential privacy implications of using SHODAN. The information SHODAN collects may include details about devices operated by individuals or organizations. Respecting privacy rights and handling data in a responsible manner is fundamental to maintaining the integrity of OSINT investigations.

In summary, understanding SHODAN's role in OSINT investigations is crucial for OSINT professionals looking to leverage this powerful search engine effectively. SHODAN's capabilities, including scanning, searching, geolocation filtering, historical data, and vulnerability detection, provide valuable insights into internet-connected devices and services. OSINT investigators must use SHODAN responsibly, adhere to ethical principles, and respect privacy rights while harnessing its capabilities to enhance their investigations in the ever-evolving digital landscape.

Chapter 2: Setting Up Your SHODAN CLI Environment

Installing and configuring SHODAN CLI is the first step towards harnessing the power of SHODAN's command-line interface for open-source intelligence (OSINT) investigations. SHODAN CLI is a versatile tool that allows users to access SHODAN's vast database of internet-connected devices and services directly from the command line. It offers a range of features and options for querying and retrieving data, making it an essential tool for OSINT professionals and security experts.

To begin the process of installing SHODAN CLI, users must have a SHODAN account and an API key. The API key is required for authentication and access to SHODAN's data. Users can obtain an API key by signing up for a SHODAN account on the SHODAN website.

Once the API key is obtained, the next step is to install SHODAN CLI on the user's system. SHODAN CLI is available for various operating systems, including Windows, macOS, and Linux. Installation instructions for each platform can be found on the SHODAN website or in the official SHODAN CLI documentation.

After installing SHODAN CLI, users should open a terminal or command prompt to begin the configuration process. The first command to run is "shodan init," followed by the API key obtained earlier. This command initializes the configuration and associates the API key with the SHODAN CLI installation.

Users can verify that the API key is correctly configured by running the "shodan info" command. This command displays information about the user's SHODAN account, including the number of query credits available and the current subscription status.

To further customize the configuration, SHODAN CLI provides options to set default parameters, such as search filters, output formats, and additional query options. Users can use the "shodan set" command followed by the desired configuration option and value to customize their SHODAN CLI environment.

For example, users can set default search filters to narrow down their queries based on specific criteria, such as geolocation, port numbers, or service banners. Customizing these filters can help users tailor their searches to their specific OSINT investigation requirements.

SHODAN CLI also offers advanced search operators that allow users to create complex queries directly from the command line. These operators include "AND," "OR," "NOT," and parentheses for grouping conditions. By using these operators strategically, users can construct precise queries to retrieve targeted data.

To execute a basic search using SHODAN CLI, users can run the "shodan search" command followed by the desired query terms. SHODAN CLI will then communicate with SHODAN's servers and retrieve relevant results based on the query. The results are displayed in the terminal, providing information about the devices, services, and vulnerabilities found.

Users can further refine their search results by using additional query options and filters. For example, the "--ports" option allows users to specify a range of port numbers to focus their search on specific services. Additionally, the "--country" and "--city" options enable geolocation-based filtering, which can be useful for investigations with a geographical context.

SHODAN CLI supports various output formats, including JSON, CSV, and list formats, to facilitate data analysis and reporting. Users can specify the desired output format using the "--format" option when executing a query. This flexibility allows users to tailor the output to their analysis tools and workflows.

Another valuable feature of SHODAN CLI is its ability to retrieve historical data about internet-connected devices. Users can use the "--history" option in their queries to access historical information, including changes in device attributes and vulnerabilities over time. This historical perspective can be instrumental in OSINT investigations and threat assessments.

Furthermore, SHODAN CLI allows users to save query results to local files for offline analysis and reporting. By using the "--output" option followed by a file path, users can export query results to a specified file in their chosen format. This capability streamlines the process of archiving and sharing OSINT findings.

In addition to basic searches, SHODAN CLI provides access to SHODAN's premium features, such as SHODAN Monitor and SHODAN Enterprise, through the command line. Users can use the "shodan monitor" and "shodan enterprise" commands to interact with these advanced services, enabling continuous monitoring, alerting, and integration into security operations.

Security professionals and OSINT investigators can also leverage SHODAN CLI for vulnerability assessment. By using the "--vulns" option in their queries, users can retrieve information about known vulnerabilities associated with the devices and services discovered. This information is crucial for assessing the security posture of internet-connected assets and prioritizing remediation efforts.

In summary, installing and configuring SHODAN CLI is a fundamental step in harnessing the power of SHODAN's command-line interface for OSINT investigations. With proper configuration and customization, users can execute precise queries, access historical data, and export results in various formats. SHODAN CLI provides a versatile toolset for security professionals and OSINT practitioners, enabling them to uncover valuable insights about internet-connected devices and services in the ever-evolving digital landscape.

Navigating the SHODAN Command Line Interface (CLI) is a critical skill for open-source intelligence (OSINT) professionals and security experts seeking to harness the full capabilities of SHODAN's powerful tools. The SHODAN CLI provides a command-line interface to interact with SHODAN's vast database of internet-connected devices and services, offering advanced querying and data retrieval options for OSINT investigations.

To navigate the SHODAN CLI effectively, users should begin by launching their terminal or command prompt and ensuring that SHODAN CLI is correctly installed and configured on their system. This includes setting up the necessary API key to authenticate and access SHODAN's data.

Once the configuration is in place, users can start exploring the functionalities of the SHODAN CLI by using various commands and options. A fundamental command to begin with is the "shodan search" command, which allows users to perform basic searches.

To execute a basic search, users can enter the "shodan search" command followed by their query terms. The SHODAN CLI will communicate with SHODAN's servers and retrieve relevant results based on the query provided. These results are displayed in the terminal, providing information about the devices, services, and vulnerabilities found.

Users can enhance their searches by applying additional query options and filters. For instance, the "--ports" option allows users to specify a range of port numbers to focus their search on specific services. The "--country" and "--city" options enable geolocation-based filtering, which can be valuable for investigations with a geographical context.

SHODAN CLI also supports advanced search operators, such as "AND," "OR," "NOT," and parentheses for grouping conditions. These operators enable users to create complex queries directly from the command line, allowing for precise and targeted searches.

To execute a query with advanced search operators, users can structure their search criteria using these operators and combine them to retrieve specific data points of interest. This level of flexibility allows for tailored searches to meet the requirements of various OSINT investigations.

Users can further refine their search results by applying filters that focus on specific attributes of internet-connected devices and services. For instance, the "--org" option allows users to filter results based on the organization associated with the devices, providing insights into the ownership or responsible entity behind the assets.

Additionally, the "--before" and "--after" options enable users to filter results based on timeframes, making it possible to retrieve historical data and track changes over time. This historical perspective can be invaluable for OSINT investigations and trend analysis.

To gain insights into the vulnerabilities associated with internet-connected assets, users can use the "--vulns" option in their queries. This option retrieves information about known vulnerabilities related to the devices and services discovered, facilitating security assessments and risk mitigation.

SHODAN CLI also supports geolocation-based filtering, which can be particularly useful for investigations with a geographic focus. The "--country" and "--city" options enable users to narrow down search results to specific regions or municipalities, aiding investigations that require local context.

The "--history" option allows users to access historical data about internet-connected devices. By including this option in their queries, users can retrieve information about changes in device attributes, configurations, and vulnerabilities over time. This historical perspective is crucial for understanding the evolution of technology and assessing risks.

SHODAN CLI provides a range of output formats, including JSON, CSV, and list formats, to facilitate data analysis and reporting. Users can specify the desired output format using the "--format" option when executing a query. This flexibility allows users to tailor the output to their analysis tools and workflows.

In addition to searching for internet-connected devices and services, SHODAN CLI offers access to SHODAN's premium features, such as SHODAN Monitor and SHODAN Enterprise. Users can interact with these advanced services through the command line, enabling continuous monitoring, alerting, and integration into security operations.

Users can use the "shodan monitor" and "shodan enterprise" commands to manage and interact with these premium services, extending the capabilities of SHODAN CLI to meet specific OSINT and security requirements.

Security professionals and OSINT investigators can also save query results to local files for offline analysis and reporting. By using the "--output" option followed by a file path, users can export query results in their preferred format. This capability simplifies the process of archiving and sharing OSINT findings.

Moreover, users can customize their SHODAN CLI environment by setting default parameters, such as search filters, output formats, and additional query options. The "shodan set" command followed by the desired configuration option and value allows users to tailor their SHODAN CLI experience to their specific needs.

To explore SHODAN's help documentation and access detailed information about commands and options, users can run the "shodan --help" or "shodan [command] --help" command. This provides a comprehensive reference for navigating the SHODAN CLI and using its features effectively.

In summary, navigating the SHODAN Command Line Interface (CLI) is an essential skill for OSINT professionals and security experts. With the ability to execute precise queries, apply advanced search operators, and customize output formats, SHODAN CLI empowers users to uncover valuable insights about internet-connected devices and services. By understanding the available commands and options, users can leverage SHODAN CLI to enhance their OSINT investigations in the ever-evolving digital landscape.

Chapter 3: Basic Search and Filtering Commands

Performing initial searches with SHODAN CLI is a pivotal step in any open-source intelligence (OSINT) investigation or security assessment. These initial searches serve as the foundation for gathering critical information about internet-connected devices and services. SHODAN CLI provides a command-line interface that allows users to query SHODAN's extensive database, offering a wealth of insights for OSINT professionals, cybersecurity experts, and researchers.

To initiate an initial search with SHODAN CLI, users must ensure that they have correctly installed and configured the tool on their system. Installation instructions for various operating systems, including Windows, macOS, and Linux, can be found on the official SHODAN website and in the documentation.

The initial setup also involves associating the SHODAN CLI installation with a SHODAN account and API key. The API key serves as a form of authentication, granting access to SHODAN's database. Users can obtain their API key by registering for a SHODAN account on the SHODAN website. It's essential to safeguard the API key and avoid sharing it, as it is a sensitive credential required for using SHODAN CLI.

Once the installation and configuration are complete, users can start performing initial searches by opening a terminal or command prompt and entering the appropriate SHODAN CLI commands. The most basic command for initiating a search is "shodan search," followed by the desired query terms.

For example, users can enter "shodan search webcams" to search for internet-connected webcams. The SHODAN CLI will execute the query and retrieve relevant results based on the query terms provided. These results typically include information about the devices, services, and vulnerabilities discovered during the search.

The results of the initial search are displayed in the terminal, presenting a summary of the devices and services found. Users can view details such as IP addresses, hostnames, open ports, and service banners. This information is invaluable for understanding the technology stack and configurations of internet-connected assets.

To gain deeper insights into the search results, users can apply various query options and filters. For instance, the "--ports" option allows users to specify a range of port numbers, enabling them to focus the search on specific services. By using this option, users can narrow down the results to devices that match their criteria.

Geolocation-based filtering is another powerful feature of SHODAN CLI. The "--country" and "--city" options allow users to filter results based on geographic regions, countries, or cities. This capability is particularly useful for OSINT investigations with a geographical context, as it helps identify assets in specific locations.

SHODAN CLI also supports advanced search operators, including "AND," "OR," "NOT," and parentheses for grouping conditions. These operators enable users to create complex queries directly from the command line. By using these operators strategically, users can construct precise queries to retrieve targeted data.

For example, users can use the "AND" operator to combine multiple search criteria in a single query. This approach allows users to find devices that meet all specified conditions, making the search results more refined and relevant.

To access historical data about internet-connected assets, users can include the "--history" option in their queries. This option retrieves information about changes in device attributes, configurations, and vulnerabilities over time. This historical perspective is essential for tracking the evolution of technology and assessing potential risks.

Furthermore, SHODAN CLI offers an option to retrieve information about known vulnerabilities associated with the devices and services discovered during the search. By using the "--vulns" option, users can access data about vulnerabilities and potential security risks, facilitating security assessments and mitigation efforts.

In addition to customizing search queries, SHODAN CLI allows users to choose from multiple output formats. These formats include JSON, CSV, and list formats, enabling users to tailor the output to their analysis tools and reporting needs. The "--format" option allows users to specify their preferred output format when executing a query.

Users can also save query results to local files for offline analysis and reporting. By using the "--output" option followed by a file path, users can export query results in their desired format. This feature streamlines the process of archiving findings and sharing them with colleagues or stakeholders.

Overall, performing initial searches with SHODAN CLI is a crucial step in OSINT investigations and security assessments. By leveraging the command-line interface's capabilities, users can execute precise queries, apply advanced search operators, and customize output formats. These initial searches provide a solid foundation for gathering information about internet-connected devices and services, supporting informed decision-making and risk assessment in the ever-evolving digital landscape.

Filtering and refining search results is a critical aspect of conducting effective open-source intelligence (OSINT) investigations using tools like SHODAN CLI. Once users have initiated their initial searches and retrieved a set of results, the ability to narrow down and focus on specific criteria becomes essential for obtaining valuable insights. SHODAN CLI offers a range of filtering and refining options that empower users to refine their search results to meet their investigative needs.

One of the primary filtering options available in SHODAN CLI is the ability to specify port numbers using the "--ports" option. This allows users to filter their search results based on the open ports associated with internet-connected devices. Port numbers correspond to specific services or applications, making it possible to pinpoint devices running specific services.

For example, users can include the "--ports 80,443" option in their query to focus on devices with open HTTP (port 80) and HTTPS (port 443) services. This type of filtering helps users identify web servers and secure web servers, which may be of particular interest in OSINT investigations.

Geolocation-based filtering is another valuable feature offered by SHODAN CLI. The "--country" and "--city" options enable users to narrow down their search results to specific geographic regions, countries, or cities. This functionality is essential when investigating assets that have a geographical context, such as identifying vulnerable systems within a particular country or city.

By including the "--country US" option in their query, users can restrict the search results to devices located in the United States. Similarly, the "--city New York" option narrows down the results to devices within the city of New York. Geolocation filtering provides context and precision in OSINT investigations.

SHODAN CLI also allows users to filter results based on the organization associated with internet-connected devices using the "--org" option. This can be valuable when users want to investigate assets belonging to a specific organization or entity.

For instance, including the "--org Microsoft" option in a query will retrieve results that are associated with the Microsoft organization. This filtering option aids users in identifying assets tied to particular organizations, which can be critical in threat assessments and cybersecurity investigations.

Users can further refine their search results by specifying timeframes using the "--before" and "--after" options. These options allow users to retrieve historical data about internet-connected devices and services, aiding in tracking changes over time.

Including the "--before 2022-01-01" option in a query retrieves results that were last seen before the specified date. Conversely, the "--after 2022-01-01" option retrieves results that were last seen after the specified date. Historical data provides insights into how devices have evolved and whether specific vulnerabilities have been addressed.

The "--history" option is another tool for accessing historical data about devices. It retrieves information about changes in device attributes, configurations, and vulnerabilities over time. This capability is essential for understanding the evolution of technology and assessing potential risks associated with internet-connected assets.

To gain insights into the vulnerabilities associated with the devices and services discovered, users can use the "--vulns" option in their queries. This option retrieves information about known vulnerabilities, allowing users to assess the security posture of internet-connected assets and prioritize remediation efforts.

For instance, including the "--vulns" option in a query for web servers may reveal vulnerabilities associated with those servers, helping users identify potential security risks.

Users can also leverage advanced search operators, such as "AND," "OR," and "NOT," to create complex queries that combine multiple conditions. These operators enable users to filter and refine search results based on specific criteria, enhancing the precision of their investigations.

For example, users can use the "AND" operator to combine multiple conditions, such as "--ports 80,443" and "--country US," to retrieve results that meet both criteria. This approach narrows down the results to devices with open HTTP or HTTPS services located in the United States.

SHODAN CLI provides various output formats, including JSON, CSV, and list formats, to accommodate different analysis tools and reporting requirements. Users can specify their preferred output format using the "--format" option when executing a query, allowing them to tailor the output to their specific needs.

In summary, filtering and refining search results are essential steps in open-source intelligence (OSINT) investigations using SHODAN CLI. By utilizing filtering options such as port numbers, geolocation, organization, timeframes, and vulnerabilities, users can pinpoint specific devices and services that are relevant to their investigations. The ability to create precise queries using advanced search operators further enhances the effectiveness of OSINT investigations. With access to historical data and customizable output formats, SHODAN CLI empowers users to refine their search results and uncover valuable insights about internet-connected assets in the ever-evolving digital landscape.

Chapter 4: Advanced Search Queries and Operators

Harnessing advanced search techniques is a crucial skill for open-source intelligence (OSINT) professionals and security experts seeking to maximize the effectiveness of their investigations using SHODAN CLI. While basic searches provide valuable insights, advanced search techniques enable users to uncover more specific and targeted information about internet-connected devices and services.

One of the advanced search techniques available in SHODAN CLI is the use of regular expressions within queries. Regular expressions, often referred to as regex, are powerful patterns that allow users to define complex search criteria. By including regex in their queries, users can search for patterns in service banners, IP addresses, and other attributes.

For instance, users can construct a query to search for devices with specific patterns in their service banners. The command might look like this: "shodan search --query 'banner:/^Apache.*2.4/'." This query would return results for devices with Apache 2.4 in their service banners.

Regex can also be employed to search for specific IP address ranges, such as those within a particular organization or network segment. Users can craft queries like "shodan search --query 'net:10.0.0.0/24'" to find devices within the specified IP range.

Another advanced search technique is the use of filters that target specific attributes of internet-connected devices. SHODAN CLI offers a variety of filters, including those related to SSL certificates, HTTP headers, and server software versions.

For example, users can apply filters to identify devices with expired SSL certificates or weak encryption configurations. These filters enable users to assess the security posture of internet-connected assets more effectively.

To search for devices with specific HTTP headers, users can use the "--http" filter in their queries. For instance, "shodan search --query 'http:'" would return results for devices with HTTP headers. Users can then further refine their search by specifying the desired headers or attributes.

Advanced users can take advantage of the "--searchtype" option in SHODAN CLI to perform deep searches. The "deep" search type instructs SHODAN to explore and retrieve additional information about the devices it finds, including banner information from various ports.

To use the "deep" search type, users can include the "--searchtype deep" option in their queries. This option enhances the comprehensiveness of search results by retrieving more detailed information about the devices and services discovered.

Furthermore, users can harness the power of SHODAN's query language to create intricate search queries. SHODAN's query language allows users to express complex conditions and combinations of filters, enabling highly customized searches.

For instance, users can create a query that searches for devices with specific ports open, running specific software versions, and located in particular geographic regions. The query might resemble: "shodan search --query 'port:80,443 product:Apache city:'."

Additionally, SHODAN CLI supports the use of the "stats" command, which provides statistical information about search results. The "stats" command can be used to summarize the data retrieved during a search, including counts of devices based on various attributes, such as port numbers, organizations, and countries.

To execute the "stats" command, users can simply append it to their search query. For example, "shodan search --query 'port:80' stats" would provide statistics about devices with port 80 open.

Users can also perform searches that target specific IoT (Internet of Things) devices and vulnerabilities. IoT devices are becoming increasingly prevalent and represent a significant area of interest for security professionals and researchers.

To search for IoT devices, users can utilize SHODAN CLI's IoT-specific filters and queries. For instance, users can run queries like "shodan search --query 'category:IoT'" to retrieve results that pertain specifically to IoT devices. This approach streamlines the identification of IoT devices within SHODAN's database.

Moreover, users can search for devices with known vulnerabilities by including the "--vulns" option in their queries. This option retrieves information about vulnerabilities associated with the devices and services discovered. It's a valuable technique for identifying potentially risky assets and prioritizing security assessments.

To harness advanced search techniques effectively, users should experiment with different combinations of filters, regular expressions, and query language expressions. This iterative approach allows users to refine their search queries and uncover increasingly precise and relevant information about internet-connected assets.

In summary, harnessing advanced search techniques in SHODAN CLI empowers users to perform more focused and insightful open-source intelligence (OSINT) investigations. By incorporating regular expressions, deep searches, specific filters, and the query language, users can create highly customized queries that reveal targeted information about internet-connected devices and services. This level of granularity is invaluable for security assessments, threat analysis, and staying informed about the ever-evolving digital landscape.

Using operators for precise queries is a fundamental skill for open-source intelligence (OSINT) professionals and security experts seeking to extract valuable insights from SHODAN CLI. Operators are powerful tools that enable users to construct complex search queries, combining various conditions and criteria to pinpoint specific internet-connected devices and services.

One of the primary operators in SHODAN CLI is the "AND" operator, which allows users to require that multiple conditions be met simultaneously in their queries. By using "AND," users can create precise queries that filter results based on multiple criteria.

For example, users can construct a query like "shodan search --query 'port:80 AND country:US'" to retrieve results for devices with port 80 open in the United States. The "AND" operator ensures that only devices meeting both conditions are included in the search results.

Conversely, the "OR" operator offers flexibility by allowing users to search for devices that meet at least one of several specified conditions. Users can construct queries like "shodan search --query 'port:80 OR port:443'" to retrieve results for devices with either port 80 or port 443 open.

The "OR" operator broadens the scope of the query, making it useful when users want to consider multiple possibilities or scenarios in their investigations.

Another valuable operator in SHODAN CLI is the "NOT" operator, which allows users to exclude specific conditions from their queries. By using "NOT," users can refine their searches by excluding results that match unwanted criteria.

For example, users can create a query like "shodan search -- query 'port:80 NOT country:CN'" to retrieve results for devices with port 80 open but exclude devices located in China. The "NOT" operator helps users filter out results that do not align with their investigation goals.

Users can combine multiple operators within a single query to create highly customized and precise searches. For instance, users can construct a query like "shodan search -- query 'port:80 AND city:New York OR city:Los Angeles NOT country:CN'" to retrieve results for devices with port 80 open in either New York or Los Angeles but exclude devices located in China.

This combination of operators allows users to express complex conditions and criteria in their queries, enabling them to uncover specific information about internet-connected assets.

SHODAN CLI also supports the use of parentheses to group conditions and control the order of operations in queries. This feature is particularly useful when constructing queries with multiple operators.

For example, users can create a query like "shodan search -- query '(port:80 OR port:443) AND country:US'" to retrieve results for devices with either port 80 or port 443 open specifically in the United States. By using parentheses, users can ensure that the "OR" condition is evaluated before the "AND" condition, affecting the query's logic.

Additionally, users can employ wildcards to broaden their search criteria when necessary. The wildcard character "*" represents any sequence of characters in a query.

For instance, users can run a query like "shodan search -- query 'product:Apache*'" to retrieve results for devices running any version of the Apache web server. This wildcard-based approach allows users to include variations of product names in their searches, accommodating different configurations and versions.

Users can also leverage the "FACET" operator to perform faceted searches and retrieve aggregated data based on specific attributes. Faceted searches are useful when users want to obtain statistics about search results.

To execute a faceted search, users can append the "FACET" operator to their query along with the attribute they want to aggregate. For example, "shodan search --query 'port:80 FACET product'" would return aggregated data about the product names associated with devices having port 80 open.

The ability to use operators for precise queries is essential for OSINT professionals and security experts seeking to extract meaningful and actionable information from SHODAN CLI. By mastering the "AND," "OR," "NOT," and "FACET" operators, as well as understanding the role of parentheses and wildcards, users can create queries that match their investigative goals with precision. These advanced querying techniques empower users to uncover specific insights about internet-connected devices and services, ultimately enhancing their ability to make informed decisions in the ever-evolving digital landscape.

Chapter 5: Monitoring Devices and Services

Real-time device monitoring with SHODAN is a powerful capability that allows open-source intelligence (OSINT) professionals and security experts to stay vigilant in the ever-changing digital landscape. By harnessing SHODAN's real-time monitoring features, users can gain immediate insights into newly discovered internet-connected devices and services, enabling them to respond proactively to emerging threats and vulnerabilities.

To initiate real-time monitoring with SHODAN, users can leverage the "stream" command provided by SHODAN CLI. The "stream" command allows users to subscribe to a continuous stream of real-time data, receiving updates as soon as new devices and services are discovered by SHODAN.

The basic syntax for starting a real-time stream is "shodan stream." By running this command, users establish a connection to SHODAN's real-time data feed, and they will receive a continuous stream of JSON-formatted data in their terminal.

This real-time data feed includes information about newly indexed devices, services, and vulnerabilities, making it a valuable resource for staying informed about changes in the digital landscape.

One of the primary use cases for real-time monitoring is tracking the appearance of specific devices or services of interest. Users can create filters within their real-time stream to receive updates only for devices that meet their predefined criteria.

For example, users can construct a filter to monitor the appearance of devices with port 22 open, indicating SSH services. The filter syntax might look like this: "shodan stream --filters 'port:22'." By including this filter, users will receive real-time updates only for devices with port 22 open. Another valuable filter is based on location. Users can specify geographic regions, countries, or cities of interest to receive real-time updates for devices located in those areas. This geographic context is particularly useful for monitoring assets with regional significance.

For instance, users can create a filter to track devices within a specific city like New York: "shodan stream --filters 'city:New York'." This filter ensures that users receive real-time updates for devices located in New York.

Additionally, users can use the "service" filter to focus on specific types of services or applications. For example, users can create a filter to monitor the appearance of web servers by including the "service" filter like so: "shodan stream --filters 'service:http'."

By applying service filters, users can narrow their real-time monitoring to particular service categories that align with their investigation or security priorities.

Real-time monitoring with SHODAN CLI is not limited to tracking devices and services; it also provides updates on vulnerabilities associated with discovered assets. Users can configure filters to receive real-time notifications about newly detected vulnerabilities, enabling them to assess and respond promptly.

To monitor vulnerabilities, users can use filters like "vuln:" followed by the vulnerability identifier or keyword. For example, to track devices vulnerable to the "Heartbleed" SSL/TLS vulnerability, users can create a filter like this: "shodan stream --filters 'vuln:Heartbleed'."

This filter ensures that users receive real-time updates for devices with known Heartbleed vulnerabilities, allowing them to prioritize vulnerability management efforts.

Real-time monitoring with SHODAN CLI extends beyond the terminal, as it provides the flexibility to integrate with other tools and processes. Users can pipe the real-time stream data to external scripts or applications, enabling custom processing and alerting mechanisms.

For example, users can create a Python script that parses the real-time stream data and triggers alerts or actions based on predefined conditions. This level of automation and customization enhances the effectiveness of real-time monitoring and response efforts.

Additionally, SHODAN CLI allows users to specify the output format for real-time stream data, facilitating integration with third-party tools and systems. Users can use the "--format" option followed by the desired format, such as JSON or CSV, to structure the real-time data feed according to their requirements.

The ability to monitor real-time data with SHODAN CLI empowers users to stay proactive in identifying and addressing potential security risks and vulnerabilities. It facilitates early detection of new devices, services, and vulnerabilities, enabling organizations to respond swiftly to emerging threats.

Furthermore, real-time monitoring supports threat intelligence and research activities, providing insights into the evolving digital landscape. OSINT professionals can leverage this capability to track the expansion of specific technologies, services, or organizations, enhancing their understanding of the online ecosystem.

In summary, real-time device monitoring with SHODAN CLI is a valuable asset for OSINT professionals, security experts, and organizations seeking to maintain a proactive security posture. By subscribing to real-time streams, creating custom filters, and integrating with external tools, users can receive timely updates about newly discovered devices, services, and vulnerabilities. This capability enhances situational awareness and empowers organizations to respond effectively to emerging threats and changes in the digital environment.

Tracking changes and updates in the ever-evolving digital landscape is a critical task for open-source intelligence (OSINT) professionals and security experts aiming to maintain situational awareness and respond effectively to emerging threats. By monitoring and analyzing alterations in devices, services, and vulnerabilities, users can stay informed and take proactive measures to protect their organizations and assets.

One of the primary methods for tracking changes and updates is through continuous scanning and monitoring of the digital environment. Tools like SHODAN CLI provide capabilities for periodic scans and assessments, allowing users to detect modifications in internet-connected devices and services over time.

To initiate regular scans with SHODAN CLI, users can use the "scan" command followed by the target or query they want to scan. For example, the command "shodan scan 'port:80'" triggers a scan for devices with port 80 open. Users can schedule these scans at intervals that suit their monitoring requirements.

Scheduled scans enable users to identify changes in device availability, service configurations, and other attributes. By comparing scan results over time, users can observe trends, patterns, and anomalies in their digital footprint.

Moreover, users can leverage SHODAN CLI's "diff" command to compare two scan results and identify differences between them. The "diff" command is particularly valuable for tracking changes in devices, services, and vulnerabilities between two specific points in time.

To execute a comparison, users can run the "diff" command with the scan IDs of the two scans they want to compare. For instance, "shodan diff 123456 789012" compares the scan results between scan ID 123456 and scan ID 789012.

The "diff" command provides detailed information about added, removed, or modified devices, services, and attributes. This feature is crucial for monitoring the evolution of the digital landscape and identifying new developments.

Additionally, users can create alerts and notifications to stay informed about specific changes and updates. SHODAN CLI allows users to set up alerts based on custom criteria, such as the appearance of devices or services matching predefined conditions.

To create an alert, users can use the "alert" command followed by the desired filter and criteria. For example, "shodan alert 'port:22'" creates an alert to notify users when devices with port 22 open are discovered.

Once alerts are configured, users receive notifications via email or other designated channels when the specified conditions are met during scans. This proactive approach to tracking changes ensures that users stay informed and can respond promptly to relevant developments.

Another method for tracking changes and updates is by monitoring vulnerabilities associated with internet-connected devices and services. Vulnerabilities are continuously discovered and reported, making it essential to keep abreast of new information.

Users can leverage SHODAN CLI's "vuln" command to access information about vulnerabilities and their associated devices. The "vuln" command allows users to search for specific vulnerabilities and retrieve details about affected assets.

For example, users can run the "vuln" command with the vulnerability identifier to obtain information about devices vulnerable to a particular security issue. This command helps users identify assets that require immediate attention or remediation efforts.

Furthermore, users can create vulnerability alerts to receive notifications when new vulnerabilities are detected in their digital footprint. By using the "alert" command with vulnerability criteria, users can set up alerts to stay informed about newly reported vulnerabilities that affect their assets.

For instance, "shodan alert 'vuln:Heartbleed'" creates an alert to notify users when new Heartbleed vulnerabilities are discovered within their scope of interest.

Tracking changes and updates also extends to monitoring the availability and status of services and applications. Users can employ SHODAN CLI's "ping" command to perform continuous health checks on specific devices or services, ensuring that they remain operational and responsive.

The "ping" command allows users to send ICMP echo requests to a target device or service to assess its availability and response times. By incorporating the "ping" command into automated scripts or monitoring systems, users can track the real-time status of critical assets.

For example, users can create a script that periodically executes the "ping" command to check the availability of web servers. If a server becomes unresponsive or experiences prolonged delays, the script can trigger alerts or automated actions, enabling rapid response to potential service interruptions.

Additionally, users can utilize SHODAN CLI's "history" command to access historical data about devices, services, and vulnerabilities. The "history" command retrieves information about changes in attributes, configurations, and vulnerabilities over time.

By analyzing historical data, users can gain insights into the evolution of technology and identify trends and patterns in the digital landscape. This information is valuable for assessing the impact of changes and updates and making informed decisions regarding security and risk management.

In summary, tracking changes and updates is a fundamental practice for OSINT professionals and security experts seeking to maintain awareness of developments in the digital environment. Continuous scanning, diff comparisons, alerts, vulnerability monitoring, and service health checks are essential techniques for staying informed about modifications in devices, services, and vulnerabilities.

These methods empower users to respond proactively to emerging threats, ensure the operational integrity of critical assets, and make data-driven decisions in the ever-evolving digital landscape. By incorporating these monitoring and tracking practices into their security and intelligence strategies, organizations and individuals can enhance their resilience and security posture.

Chapter 6: Shodan Exploits and Vulnerability Assessment

Identifying vulnerabilities in devices is a fundamental task for cybersecurity professionals, as it forms the basis of effective threat mitigation and risk management strategies. The process of identifying vulnerabilities involves assessing hardware, software, and configurations to uncover weaknesses that malicious actors could exploit. One of the primary methods for identifying vulnerabilities in devices is through vulnerability scanning and assessment tools. These tools, often automated, systematically examine devices, networks, and systems to detect known vulnerabilities and weaknesses.

A widely used vulnerability scanning tool is Nessus, which enables users to scan devices for a broad range of known vulnerabilities. By running Nessus scans, security professionals can identify vulnerabilities that pose risks to the security and functionality of devices.

To use Nessus effectively, users can run scans with specific profiles and configurations tailored to their needs. For instance, a user can run a scan with a "Web Application" profile to focus on vulnerabilities associated with web applications or a "Compliance" profile to assess device compliance with industry standards and regulations.

Another popular vulnerability assessment tool is OpenVAS (Open Vulnerability Assessment System), which provides an open-source framework for vulnerability scanning and management. OpenVAS offers a range of scanning capabilities, including network vulnerability scans and web application security testing.

Users can initiate OpenVAS scans by configuring scan tasks, selecting target devices or networks, and specifying scan preferences. The tool then conducts comprehensive vulnerability assessments and generates reports highlighting identified vulnerabilities.

Beyond automated scanning tools, manual vulnerability assessments play a crucial role in identifying vulnerabilities. Manual assessments involve in-depth examination and testing of devices and configurations by cybersecurity experts.

Security professionals can use a variety of techniques during manual assessments, such as penetration testing, code review, and configuration analysis. These methods allow experts to uncover vulnerabilities that automated tools may overlook or fail to detect.

For example, during a penetration test, a cybersecurity professional may attempt to exploit potential vulnerabilities to assess the device's resistance to attacks. This hands-on approach simulates real-world threat scenarios and helps identify vulnerabilities that could lead to security breaches.

Furthermore, code review involves examining the source code of software and firmware to identify coding errors, logical flaws, and vulnerabilities. This technique is particularly relevant for assessing vulnerabilities in custom or proprietary applications and firmware.

Configuration analysis, on the other hand, focuses on reviewing device configurations and settings to ensure they align with security best practices and compliance requirements. Security experts analyze configurations to identify misconfigurations or weak security settings that could expose devices to vulnerabilities.

The process of identifying vulnerabilities also extends to vulnerability databases and sources of security intelligence. Cybersecurity professionals regularly consult databases like the Common Vulnerabilities and Exposures (CVE) system, the National Vulnerability Database (NVD), and vendor-specific security advisories to stay informed about newly discovered vulnerabilities.

By monitoring these sources, professionals can access detailed information about vulnerabilities, including their severity, impact, affected devices, and available patches or mitigations. This knowledge is crucial for prioritizing vulnerability remediation efforts and making informed decisions regarding device security.

Furthermore, organizations and security teams can subscribe to vulnerability notification services, such as the National Cyber Awareness System (NCAS), to receive timely alerts about newly discovered vulnerabilities that may affect their devices and systems.

Identifying vulnerabilities also involves the assessment of device configurations and security settings. Security professionals can use configuration assessment tools and security baselines to evaluate devices against established security standards and guidelines.

For instance, the Center for Internet Security (CIS) provides security baselines and benchmarks for various operating systems and applications. Organizations can use these baselines as reference points for assessing the security posture of their devices.

Automated configuration assessment tools, such as the Security Content Automation Protocol (SCAP) tools, facilitate the evaluation of device configurations against security profiles and standards. These tools generate reports highlighting configuration deviations and potential vulnerabilities. Additionally, vulnerability identification encompasses the assessment of third-party software and components used in devices. Many devices rely on third-party libraries, frameworks, and software components, which may contain known vulnerabilities.

Security professionals can employ software composition analysis (SCA) tools to identify vulnerabilities in third-party software dependencies. These tools scan device software and firmware to detect outdated or vulnerable components and provide recommendations for remediation. Furthermore, continuous monitoring and assessment are essential for maintaining device security. Vulnerabilities may emerge or evolve over time due to software updates, new attack techniques, or changes in device configurations. To address this, organizations should establish a vulnerability management program that includes periodic scanning, assessment, and remediation. Vulnerability management practices involve the identification, prioritization, and mitigation of vulnerabilities based on their criticality and potential impact. The process of identifying vulnerabilities in devices is an ongoing effort that requires a combination of automated scanning, manual assessment, monitoring of security intelligence sources, and adherence to security standards. By implementing comprehensive vulnerability identification practices, organizations can enhance their device security, reduce risks, and respond effectively to emerging threats in an ever-changing cybersecurity landscape. Exploiting vulnerable services safely is a crucial skill for ethical hackers, penetration testers, and security professionals seeking to assess and improve the security of systems and networks. The goal of safe exploitation is to identify and demonstrate vulnerabilities without causing harm or disruption to the targeted system or network. To achieve this, security practitioners follow a set of best practices and ethical guidelines. One of the fundamental principles of safe exploitation is obtaining proper authorization. Before attempting to exploit vulnerabilities, ethical hackers must have explicit permission from the system owner or administrator. Unauthorized penetration testing or exploitation can lead to legal consequences and damage trust.

Once authorized, ethical hackers perform reconnaissance to gather information about the target system or network. Reconnaissance includes identifying the services, software versions, and configurations in use. This information is essential for selecting appropriate exploitation techniques.

A critical aspect of safe exploitation is the use of responsible disclosure practices. If ethical hackers discover vulnerabilities during their assessments, they should report them to the system owner or vendor promptly, following established disclosure procedures. Responsible disclosure helps ensure that vulnerabilities are addressed and mitigated, contributing to overall security.

Ethical hackers should use dedicated lab environments or controlled test systems for safe exploitation. These environments mimic real-world systems but are isolated and separated from production systems to prevent unintended consequences.

In safe exploitation, it's vital to prioritize testing and exploitation techniques that minimize the risk of system instability or data loss. Ethical hackers select techniques that have a low impact on the target system's stability and integrity.

For example, when assessing web applications, ethical hackers might start with SQL injection tests that retrieve data without modifying it, instead of attempting destructive attacks like data deletion.

Using non-intrusive scanning and testing methods is a key practice in safe exploitation. These methods aim to identify vulnerabilities without actively exploiting them. Non-intrusive techniques, such as vulnerability scanning and passive information gathering, reduce the risk of accidental system disruption.

In safe exploitation, ethical hackers leverage tools and scripts that are well-tested and reliable. Using unverified or potentially unstable tools can introduce unexpected issues and lead to unintended consequences.

Ethical hackers should also exercise caution when testing zero-day vulnerabilities or previously unknown weaknesses. Testing zero-day vulnerabilities can be risky because there may be limited information available about them, increasing the likelihood of unintended outcomes.

Safe exploitation involves thorough testing and validation of vulnerabilities. Ethical hackers conduct careful testing to ensure that identified vulnerabilities can be consistently exploited and verified. They avoid one-time or unreliable exploitation attempts.

Furthermore, safe exploitation practices include documenting the steps taken and the results obtained during the assessment. Documentation provides a clear record of the vulnerabilities identified, their impact, and the successful exploitation techniques used. This documentation is essential for reporting and remediation.

When exploiting vulnerabilities, ethical hackers follow the principle of "do no harm." They refrain from actions that could disrupt services, damage data, or harm the integrity of the target system. Instead, their focus is on demonstrating the vulnerability's existence and potential impact.

Ethical hackers always maintain professionalism and integrity during the exploitation process. They adhere to a code of ethics that emphasizes honesty, transparency, and respect for privacy and legal boundaries. This ensures that their actions align with ethical standards and legal requirements.

In addition to safe exploitation, ethical hackers are responsible for providing recommendations and guidance for mitigating identified vulnerabilities. They assist system owners and administrators in understanding the risks and implementing effective security measures.

Ethical hackers often deliver detailed reports that outline the vulnerabilities discovered, their potential impact, and recommended remediation steps. These reports help organizations improve their security posture and protect their systems from potential threats.

To summarize, safe exploitation is a critical aspect of ethical hacking and security assessments. It involves obtaining proper authorization, responsible disclosure, using controlled environments, prioritizing non-intrusive methods, and adhering to ethical guidelines. Ethical hackers prioritize system stability and integrity while identifying vulnerabilities and providing valuable insights for security improvement.

Chapter 7: Custom Scripts and Automation with SHODAN

Creating custom SHODAN scripts is an advanced skill that allows security professionals and researchers to automate and tailor SHODAN queries and data retrieval to their specific needs.

Custom SHODAN scripts are typically written in programming languages such as Python, Ruby, or JavaScript, using SHODAN's API (Application Programming Interface) to interact with SHODAN's database and retrieve information about devices, services, and vulnerabilities.

One of the primary reasons for creating custom SHODAN scripts is to streamline and automate the process of querying SHODAN for specific information. Instead of manually entering queries through the SHODAN website or CLI, custom scripts enable users to define complex search criteria and retrieve results programmatically.

To get started with creating custom SHODAN scripts, users need to obtain an API key from SHODAN. The API key is necessary for authenticating and accessing SHODAN's API services. Users can sign up for a SHODAN account and generate an API key from their account settings.

Once the API key is obtained, users can integrate it into their custom scripts by including it in the script's authentication process. The API key serves as the authentication token that allows the script to access SHODAN's API services.

Custom SHODAN scripts can be designed to perform various tasks, depending on the specific requirements. Some common use cases include searching for devices with specific open ports, identifying vulnerable services, tracking changes in device configurations, and monitoring real-time data.

For example, a custom script can be created to search for all devices with port 22 (SSH) open within a specified geographic area. The script would use the SHODAN API to execute the search query and retrieve the results, which can then be processed and analyzed as needed.

To create custom SHODAN scripts, users typically choose a programming language that they are familiar with and comfortable using. Python is a popular choice due to its ease of use, extensive libraries, and support for making HTTP requests to interact with SHODAN's API.

In Python, users can use the "requests" library to send HTTP requests to SHODAN's API endpoints. The script can be structured to send a search query to SHODAN's API and receive the response in JSON format, which can then be parsed and processed within the script.

Custom SHODAN scripts can also incorporate error handling and exception management to ensure that the script operates smoothly, even when encountering issues such as network errors or API rate limits. Handling exceptions gracefully helps maintain the reliability and stability of the script.

Furthermore, custom SHODAN scripts can be designed to retrieve detailed information about discovered devices, services, and vulnerabilities. This information can include IP addresses, hostnames, banners, software versions, and even historical data about changes and updates.

Users can implement filtering and sorting mechanisms within their scripts to refine the search results and focus on the most relevant information. This allows for efficient data analysis and decision-making based on the retrieved data.

In addition to querying SHODAN's database, custom scripts can be used to automate specific tasks related to vulnerability assessment and threat intelligence. For example, a custom script can periodically check for devices vulnerable to a known CVE (Common Vulnerabilities and Exposures) and provide alerts when such devices are discovered.

Moreover, custom SHODAN scripts can integrate with other security tools and systems, enhancing their capabilities. For instance, a custom script can be part of a larger security automation framework that orchestrates vulnerability scanning, patch management, and incident response based on SHODAN data.

It's important to note that while custom SHODAN scripts offer significant flexibility and automation, they should be used responsibly and ethically. Users must ensure that their scripts comply with SHODAN's terms of service and respect the privacy and legal boundaries of the devices and networks they interact with.

Additionally, users should be aware of SHODAN's API rate limits, which restrict the number of requests that can be made within a specific timeframe. Proper rate limiting and error handling should be implemented in custom scripts to avoid exceeding these limits and disrupting API access.

In summary, creating custom SHODAN scripts is a valuable skill for security professionals and researchers seeking to automate and customize their interactions with SHODAN's database. Custom scripts can streamline data retrieval, support various use cases, and enhance security operations by integrating with other tools and systems.

However, users must exercise responsibility and adhere to ethical guidelines when developing and using custom SHODAN scripts.

Automating routine OSINT (Open Source Intelligence) tasks is a valuable practice that can significantly enhance the efficiency and effectiveness of intelligence gathering and analysis processes.

Automation in OSINT involves the use of scripts, tools, and workflows to perform repetitive tasks and collect information from various sources, such as websites, social media, and online databases.

One of the primary benefits of automating routine OSINT tasks is time savings. By automating tasks that would otherwise require manual intervention, analysts can allocate more time to higher-level analysis and decision-making activities.

To begin automating OSINT tasks, analysts often start by identifying the specific tasks and processes that are repetitive and time-consuming. These tasks can range from web scraping and data extraction to social media monitoring and keyword analysis.

For example, a common OSINT task is monitoring news websites and blogs for mentions of specific keywords or topics relevant to an investigation. Instead of manually checking multiple websites daily, automation scripts can be created to scrape and collect articles containing the target keywords.

Python, a versatile programming language, is often used for creating automation scripts in OSINT. Python offers libraries and modules for web scraping, data manipulation, and working with APIs, making it a suitable choice for OSINT automation.

In Python, analysts can use libraries like BeautifulSoup and Requests to scrape web content, while modules like pandas can help organize and analyze collected data. Additionally, APIs provided by online platforms, such as Twitter or Reddit, can be integrated into scripts for real-time data retrieval.

Automation scripts can be tailored to specific OSINT use cases. For instance, in a threat intelligence context, analysts may create scripts to monitor social media platforms for mentions of specific threat actors, malware, or attack techniques.

In this scenario, the script would continuously query social media APIs for relevant posts and analyze the content to extract relevant information, such as indicators of compromise (IOCs) or insights into emerging threats.

Furthermore, automation can aid in the tracking of domain registrations, DNS changes, and SSL certificate updates. By regularly querying domain registration databases and certificate transparency logs, analysts can detect suspicious or unauthorized changes related to potential cyber threats or phishing campaigns.

Automation can also be applied to monitoring online forums, discussion boards, and dark web communities for discussions related to specific topics or keywords. This approach can help identify emerging trends, discussions about vulnerabilities, and potential threats.

As part of automation, analysts can leverage regular expressions and natural language processing (NLP) techniques to extract valuable insights from unstructured text data. NLP tools can identify patterns, sentiment, and entities mentioned in text, enhancing the analysis of OSINT data.

Additionally, analysts can use automation to aggregate data from multiple sources into centralized repositories or dashboards. Tools like Elasticsearch and Kibana can be employed to index and visualize OSINT data, providing a unified view for analysis and reporting.

Automation also facilitates the creation of alerts and notifications. Analysts can set up automated alerts to notify them when specific events or conditions are met, such as the appearance of new mentions of keywords or changes in online forums related to a particular threat actor.

Furthermore, automation can assist in data enrichment by retrieving additional context and metadata about collected information. For instance, automated processes can resolve IP addresses to geolocations, identify ownership of domains, and cross-reference data against known threat intelligence feeds.

Automation scripts can be scheduled to run at specific intervals, ensuring that OSINT data is continuously updated and analyzed. Regular updates enable analysts to stay informed about changes, trends, and potential threats in real-time.

However, it's important to exercise caution when automating OSINT tasks, as certain actions may violate terms of service or acceptable use policies of online platforms. Analysts should review and comply with the rules and regulations of the sources they are collecting data from.

In summary, automating routine OSINT tasks is a powerful approach to enhance the efficiency and effectiveness of intelligence gathering and analysis. Automation enables analysts to save time, monitor multiple sources simultaneously, and extract valuable insights from vast amounts of data.

By identifying repetitive tasks, selecting the appropriate automation tools and techniques, and adhering to ethical and legal guidelines, OSINT professionals can streamline their workflows and improve their ability to detect, analyze, and respond to emerging threats and intelligence needs.

Chapter 8: Using SHODAN for IoT and Industrial Control Systems

Discovering IoT (Internet of Things) devices and infrastructure is a crucial aspect of modern cybersecurity and network monitoring efforts. As the IoT ecosystem continues to expand, understanding how to identify, assess, and manage IoT devices becomes increasingly important.

IoT devices encompass a wide range of interconnected devices, including smart thermostats, cameras, wearables, industrial sensors, and more. These devices communicate with each other and central systems over the internet, creating a complex network of interconnected components.

Discovering IoT devices and infrastructure involves several key processes and techniques. One of the primary methods is network scanning and enumeration, which helps identify active devices and open ports on a network.

Tools like Nmap, for example, allow network administrators and security professionals to conduct comprehensive scans of their networks to identify devices, open ports, and services. By scanning the network, it becomes possible to detect IoT devices and their associated services.

Another approach to discovering IoT devices is through the analysis of network traffic. Network traffic analysis tools, such as Wireshark, can capture and inspect data packets passing through the network. Analysts can look for patterns and signatures indicative of IoT device communication.

IoT devices often use specific communication protocols and standards, such as MQTT (Message Queuing Telemetry Transport) or CoAP (Constrained Application Protocol). Recognizing these protocols in network traffic can be a strong indicator of IoT device presence.

Additionally, network monitoring tools can help detect unusual or unauthorized IoT device behavior. Anomalies in data traffic, unusual connection patterns, or unexpected data transfers may signal the presence of rogue IoT devices or security breaches.

Furthermore, organizations can leverage IoT discovery platforms and solutions designed specifically for identifying and managing IoT devices on their networks. These platforms provide visibility into the IoT ecosystem, enabling administrators to track devices, monitor their status, and assess their security posture.

An important consideration in discovering IoT devices is the need for device authentication and access control. Unauthorized or poorly secured IoT devices can pose significant security risks. Implementing strong authentication mechanisms and access controls helps prevent unauthorized access and misuse of IoT devices.

Command-line tools and scripts can be employed to query and interact with IoT devices on a network. For example, the "mosquitto_pub" command can be used to publish messages to MQTT brokers, allowing administrators to communicate with IoT devices using the MQTT protocol.

In addition to network discovery, physical inspection of the environment can aid in identifying IoT devices. For example, in industrial settings, IoT sensors and actuators may be physically connected to machinery or equipment.

Identifying and cataloging these physical devices can be essential for network mapping and security.

Another critical aspect of discovering IoT devices is the utilization of specialized scanning tools designed for IoT device identification. Some security tools and scanners are tailored to identify common IoT devices, their vulnerabilities, and potential misconfigurations.

IoT device manufacturers often assign unique MAC (Media Access Control) addresses to their devices. These addresses can be used to identify and categorize IoT devices on a network. Tools like "arp-scan" can assist in mapping MAC addresses to specific device manufacturers and models.

Furthermore, IoT devices may have default credentials or vulnerabilities that can be exploited by malicious actors. Identifying such devices early on allows organizations to secure them and reduce the risk of compromise.

Regular device inventory audits and monitoring are essential for maintaining an accurate record of IoT devices within an organization. As IoT environments evolve and devices are added or removed, continuous discovery efforts ensure that the network remains secure and well-managed.

For comprehensive IoT discovery, it's important to consider both on-premises and cloud-based IoT devices. Many organizations are adopting cloud-based IoT solutions, and these devices may not be present on the local network. Cloud monitoring and management tools are necessary for tracking and securing these devices.

In summary, discovering IoT devices and infrastructure is a critical component of modern cybersecurity and network management. Organizations must employ a combination of network scanning, traffic analysis, physical inspection, and specialized tools to identify, assess, and secure IoT devices on their networks.

By maintaining a comprehensive inventory of IoT devices, implementing strong authentication and access controls, and staying vigilant for potential security risks, organizations can effectively manage and secure their IoT ecosystems in an evolving and interconnected world.

Assessing security risks in industrial systems is a critical endeavor in today's interconnected world, where industries rely heavily on digital technologies and automation to streamline operations and improve efficiency.

Industrial systems encompass a wide range of critical infrastructure, including manufacturing plants, power generation facilities, water treatment plants, and transportation networks. These systems are increasingly connected to the internet and often referred to as Industrial Control Systems (ICS) or Operational Technology (OT) environments.

To assess security risks in industrial systems effectively, it is essential to begin with a comprehensive understanding of the unique challenges and complexities that these environments present. Industrial systems are designed to operate reliably and efficiently, with a focus on safety and uptime, which sometimes results in security being a secondary consideration.

One of the primary challenges in assessing security risks in industrial systems is the presence of legacy and legacy-like systems. Many industrial facilities still use legacy equipment and technologies that were not designed with modern cybersecurity in mind. These systems may lack essential security features and receive limited updates or patches.

Another challenge is the convergence of IT (Information Technology) and OT (Operational Technology) networks. As organizations seek to improve operational efficiency and data analytics, IT and OT environments are increasingly interconnected. However, this convergence introduces potential vulnerabilities and attack surfaces that need careful assessment.

Security assessments in industrial systems often begin with a thorough inventory of assets. Understanding what devices and systems are present in the environment is crucial for identifying potential weaknesses. Tools like network scanners, asset discovery solutions, and manual inspections can help create an accurate asset inventory.

Vulnerability scanning is another essential component of assessing security risks in industrial systems. Vulnerability scanners, like Nessus or OpenVAS, can identify known vulnerabilities in devices and software present in the industrial environment. Regular scans help keep the security posture up to date.

Penetration testing is a valuable technique for assessing security risks. Penetration testers simulate real-world attacks to identify weaknesses in the system's defenses. They may attempt to exploit vulnerabilities and gain unauthorized access to demonstrate potential risks and vulnerabilities that require mitigation.

In addition to technical assessments, evaluating the effectiveness of security policies and procedures is crucial. Organizations should assess their security policies, incident response plans, and access controls to ensure they align with industry best practices and regulatory requirements.

Asset criticality assessments are essential in prioritizing security efforts. Not all assets within an industrial environment are equally critical. Identifying which assets are most vital to the operation and safety of the system helps organizations focus their security resources on protecting these assets first.

Security assessments in industrial systems should also consider insider threats. Insiders with malicious intent or inadvertently making mistakes can pose significant risks. Implementing user behavior analytics and monitoring for abnormal activities can help detect insider threats.

Furthermore, evaluating the security of remote access and external connections is essential. Many industrial systems allow remote access for maintenance and monitoring, which can be exploited by attackers if not adequately secured. Assessing the security of remote access methods and connections is critical.

Security assessments in industrial systems should also include a review of network segmentation and access controls. Properly segmenting the network and controlling access between different segments can limit the potential impact of a security breach.

Intrusion detection and prevention systems (IDS/IPS) are valuable tools for real-time monitoring and alerting. These systems can detect and respond to suspicious activities, helping organizations respond promptly to security incidents.

Regular security training and awareness programs for employees are vital. Educating staff on security best practices, such as recognizing phishing attempts or reporting suspicious activities, can significantly reduce security risks.

Finally, organizations should consider conducting red teaming exercises. Red teaming involves hiring external experts to simulate sophisticated attacks on the industrial environment. These exercises provide a realistic assessment of the security posture and help identify weaknesses.

In summary, assessing security risks in industrial systems is a multifaceted process that requires a comprehensive understanding of the challenges and complexities of these environments. It involves inventorying assets, vulnerability scanning, penetration testing, evaluating security policies, and considering insider threats.

Securing industrial systems is an ongoing effort that requires continuous monitoring, regular assessments, and the implementation of security best practices. As industries increasingly rely on digital technologies and connectivity, the importance of robust security measures in these environments cannot be overstated.

Chapter 9: Case Studies in OSINT Investigations with SHODAN

Analyzing real-world OSINT (Open Source Intelligence) cases provides valuable insights into the practical application of OSINT techniques and the impact of OSINT in various fields. OSINT practitioners often encounter complex challenges and diverse scenarios when conducting investigations or intelligence gathering.

One common use of OSINT is in the realm of law enforcement and cybercrime investigations. In cases involving cyberattacks, digital forensics, and online fraud, OSINT plays a crucial role in identifying suspects, tracing digital footprints, and collecting evidence from open sources.

For example, consider a case where a company falls victim to a cyberattack, resulting in a data breach. OSINT analysts may be tasked with tracing the origins of the attack, identifying the hacker or hacking group responsible, and assessing the extent of the data exposure.

In this scenario, OSINT techniques could involve analyzing publicly available data on hacking forums, underground marketplaces, and social media platforms to gather information about potential threat actors or indicators of compromise (IOCs).

The analysis may include monitoring for the sale of stolen data, tracking cryptocurrency transactions, and identifying any online discussions or bragging by the attackers. This multifaceted approach leverages OSINT to piece together a comprehensive understanding of the incident.

Another real-world application of OSINT is in the field of threat intelligence. Organizations and cybersecurity firms use OSINT to monitor and assess potential threats to their networks and infrastructure.

For instance, consider a threat intelligence team responsible for protecting a financial institution's network. They may utilize OSINT to gather information on emerging threats, malware campaigns, and vulnerabilities relevant to the financial sector.

OSINT feeds and sources, such as public reports, blogs, social media discussions, and dark web forums, are continuously monitored to stay informed about evolving threats. Analyzing these sources enables the team to proactively implement defensive measures and keep the organization secure.

OSINT is also instrumental in geopolitical analysis and national security. Government agencies and intelligence organizations employ OSINT techniques to gather information about foreign actors, geopolitical developments, and potential threats to national interests.

In a real-world geopolitical OSINT case, analysts may focus on monitoring news outlets, social media activity, and publicly available documents related to a specific region or conflict. By aggregating and analyzing these open sources, they can gain insights into the actions and intentions of foreign entities.

Moreover, OSINT is invaluable in conducting due diligence and risk assessment for businesses and financial institutions. When evaluating potential business partners, investments, or mergers and acquisitions, organizations rely on OSINT to gather information about the reputation, financial stability, and background of entities involved.

In a due diligence OSINT case, analysts may employ OSINT tools to research the public records, news articles, legal documents, and social media profiles of individuals and organizations. The goal is to uncover any red flags or hidden risks that could impact business decisions.

OSINT also plays a vital role in cybersecurity incident response. When an organization faces a security incident, such as a data breach or malware infection, OSINT is used to gather information about the threat, its tactics, techniques, and procedures (TTPs), and potential impact.

In a real-world incident response OSINT case, analysts may collect samples of malicious code or phishing emails and analyze them to identify attribution clues. They may also investigate the infrastructure used by the threat actors, such as command and control servers, domains, and IP addresses.

Additionally, OSINT can assist in identifying data leaks or exposures of sensitive information. OSINT analysts may use search engines, data breach databases, and dark web forums to discover instances where an organization's data has been exposed, helping the organization take corrective action.

OSINT is increasingly relevant in the world of online reputation management. Individuals and businesses alike rely on OSINT to monitor their online presence, track mentions, and assess their digital reputation.

In a personal reputation management OSINT case, an individual may use OSINT tools and techniques to monitor their online footprint. They can track social media mentions, online reviews, and news articles related to their name to ensure that their online image remains positive and accurate.

Moreover, OSINT has applications in competitive intelligence, market research, and brand monitoring. Organizations can use OSINT to gather information about competitors, market trends, and customer sentiment, helping them make informed business decisions.

In summary, analyzing real-world OSINT cases illustrates the versatility and importance of OSINT across various domains and industries. OSINT is a powerful tool for conducting investigations, protecting cybersecurity, monitoring geopolitical developments, performing due diligence, and managing online reputation.

Whether used by law enforcement agencies, cybersecurity professionals, intelligence organizations, or businesses, OSINT continues to prove its value in today's information-driven world, providing actionable insights and aiding decision-making processes.

Extracting insights from successful investigations is a fundamental step in the process of improving investigative techniques and optimizing future operations. It involves analyzing the methods, strategies, and outcomes of previous investigations to gain valuable knowledge and lessons learned.

One essential aspect of extracting insights from successful investigations is the documentation of the investigative process. Investigators should maintain detailed records of their activities, decisions, and findings throughout the investigation. Proper documentation ensures that the investigation can be reviewed and analyzed later.

In addition to documenting the process, investigators should also record the specific tools, techniques, and methodologies employed during the investigation. This includes any specialized software, hardware, or forensic tools used to collect and analyze evidence.

Command-line tools are often used in digital forensic investigations to extract and analyze data from electronic devices. Commands like "dd" and "foremost" can be used to create disk images and recover deleted files, while "volatility" is commonly employed to analyze memory dumps.

Another critical aspect of extracting insights from successful investigations is the analysis of the collected evidence. Investigators should thoroughly examine the data and information gathered during the investigation, looking for patterns, anomalies, and relevant details.

Analyzing the data often involves the use of specialized software and tools designed for forensic analysis. For example, "Autopsy" is an open-source digital forensic tool that assists in examining disk images, while "EnCase" provides advanced capabilities for computer and mobile device forensics.

The analysis may include the examination of file timestamps, file metadata, and file content to establish timelines and identify suspicious activities. Investigators may use regular expressions and keyword searches to locate specific information within the data.

Moreover, investigators should consider the broader context of the investigation. This involves understanding the motives and objectives of the individuals or entities involved in the case. It may also require examining the geopolitical or industry-specific factors that could have influenced the incident.

For example, in a cybersecurity investigation, understanding the motivations and tactics of threat actors is crucial. Investigators may analyze malware samples, command and control infrastructure, and communication patterns to attribute the attack to a specific threat group.

Furthermore, investigators should explore the impact of the investigation's outcomes. This includes assessing the success of the investigation in achieving its objectives, such as identifying suspects, recovering stolen assets, or mitigating security threats.

The outcomes of the investigation may also inform future actions and decisions. For instance, if the investigation led to the identification of vulnerabilities in an organization's security posture, recommendations for remediation and improved security measures may be extracted from the insights gained.

In some cases, extracting insights from successful investigations may involve collaboration with other experts or stakeholders. Peer review and feedback from colleagues can provide valuable perspectives and help identify areas for improvement.

It's important to consider the ethical and legal implications of investigations and the handling of evidence. Compliance with relevant laws, regulations, and ethical standards is essential throughout the investigative process.

Moreover, sharing the insights and lessons learned from successful investigations within an organization or across the industry can contribute to collective knowledge and enhance overall security and investigative capabilities.

In summary, extracting insights from successful investigations is a crucial component of continuous improvement in the field of investigations, whether in digital forensics, law enforcement, cybersecurity, or other domains. It involves documenting the process, analyzing evidence, understanding motives, considering context, assessing outcomes, and ensuring ethical and legal compliance.

By systematically reviewing and learning from past successes, investigators can refine their techniques, adapt to evolving threats, and contribute to the advancement of investigative practices in their respective fields.

Chapter 10: Mastering SHODAN CLI for Professional Intelligence Gathering

Advanced techniques for OSINT (Open Source Intelligence) professionals are essential for those who seek to excel in the field of intelligence gathering and investigative research. These techniques go beyond the basics and require a deep understanding of online sources, tools, and methodologies.

One advanced technique involves the use of advanced search operators when querying search engines and online databases. These operators allow OSINT professionals to refine their searches and retrieve more targeted information. For example, using the "site:" operator followed by a specific website domain restricts search results to that site, while "intitle:" can be used to find web pages with specific keywords in their titles.

Another valuable tool in the OSINT professional's toolkit is the utilization of specialized search engines and databases that focus on specific types of information. These resources provide access to data that may not be easily discoverable through conventional search engines. Examples include Shodan for searching Internet of Things (IoT) devices and Censys for network data.

Advanced OSINT professionals also leverage social media monitoring and analysis tools to extract valuable insights from social media platforms. Tools like Brandwatch and Mention allow professionals to track mentions, analyze sentiment, and identify trends across various social networks. Moreover, they can use social media analysis commands like "from:" and "to:" to filter content based on specific users or conversations.

In addition to social media, deep web and dark web investigations are advanced OSINT techniques that require specialized skills and tools. The deep web consists of web pages not indexed by traditional search engines, while the dark web is a hidden part of the internet accessible only through special software. OSINT professionals use Tor and other anonymizing tools to access the dark web, where they can gather intelligence on illicit activities and threat actors.

Furthermore, OSINT professionals often employ advanced geolocation techniques to identify the physical locations of individuals or entities. Tools like Maltego and Google Earth can assist in geolocating IP addresses, social media posts, and images. Advanced techniques involve triangulating multiple data points to narrow down the target's location accurately.

OSINT professionals also engage in open-source threat intelligence (OSTI) to proactively identify and assess potential threats. OSTI involves monitoring online forums, chat rooms, and hacker communities to gather intelligence on emerging threats, vulnerabilities, and attack methods. Advanced OSINT practitioners may use automated scripts and monitoring tools to efficiently track threat actor discussions.

Moreover, OSINT professionals with advanced skills in linguistics and natural language processing can perform sentiment analysis on text data gathered from online sources. This analysis helps in understanding public opinion, assessing the reputation of individuals or organizations, and identifying potential trends or emerging issues.

Advanced OSINT techniques also encompass the use of OSINT automation and scripting. Professionals create custom scripts and workflows to automate data collection, analysis, and reporting. Python, for instance, is a popular programming language for building OSINT automation scripts, enabling the extraction of data from various sources and the generation of comprehensive reports.

Furthermore, OSINT professionals with advanced knowledge of digital forensics can analyze digital evidence obtained from online sources. They use forensic tools and techniques to examine artifacts, recover deleted data, and reconstruct digital activities. Digital forensics commands such as "volatility" and "autopsy" are essential for deep analysis.

Advanced OSINT practitioners often engage in target profiling and social engineering assessments. They gather extensive information about a target, including personal details, online behaviors, and preferences. This information can be used for various purposes, including threat assessments, vulnerability identification, and penetration testing.

Advanced OSINT techniques also involve OSINT fusion and analysis. OSINT professionals integrate data from multiple sources, including open-source intelligence, human intelligence, and signals intelligence, to create a comprehensive intelligence picture. Advanced analysts employ analytical techniques like link analysis and network analysis to uncover hidden connections and patterns within the data.

In summary, advanced techniques for OSINT professionals encompass a wide range of skills, tools, and methodologies. These techniques go beyond basic information gathering and require a deep understanding of advanced search operators, specialized search engines, social media monitoring, deep web and dark web investigations, geolocation, open-source threat intelligence, sentiment analysis, automation, digital forensics, target profiling, social engineering assessments, and OSINT fusion and analysis.

By mastering these advanced techniques, OSINT professionals can enhance their capabilities in intelligence gathering, threat assessment, and investigative research, ultimately contributing to improved decision-making and security measures. Strategies for continuous improvement in intelligence gathering are essential for individuals and organizations aiming to stay ahead in an ever-evolving information landscape. These strategies involve a proactive approach to enhancing intelligence gathering processes, methodologies, and outcomes.

One fundamental strategy is to establish a culture of learning and adaptability within the intelligence community. This culture encourages professionals to seek out new knowledge, skills, and techniques continually. Command-line tools like "man" and "help" can be used to access documentation and learn about the capabilities and options of various tools. Moreover, organizations should invest in ongoing training and professional development programs for intelligence professionals. These programs help keep practitioners updated on the latest advancements in intelligence gathering methods and technologies. Online courses and certifications can be valuable resources for individuals looking to expand their skills. Another key strategy is to embrace technological advancements in intelligence gathering. The field of information technology is constantly evolving, and intelligence professionals should stay informed about the latest tools and platforms. This includes exploring advanced data analytics, machine learning, and automation solutions that can streamline data collection and analysis. Incorporating automation into intelligence gathering processes can significantly enhance efficiency and effectiveness. OSINT professionals can create scripts and workflows using command-line languages like Bash and Python to automate repetitive tasks. Automation tools like "cron" can schedule tasks to run at specific intervals, ensuring continuous data collection.

Furthermore, intelligence professionals should establish robust data management practices. Proper data organization, storage, and retrieval systems are essential for maintaining the integrity and accessibility of collected information. Command-line commands like "grep" and "find" can help search for specific data within large datasets.

Strategic partnerships and collaboration with external organizations and experts are vital strategies for intelligence gathering improvement. Sharing knowledge and insights with other professionals in the field can lead to a broader understanding of emerging threats and intelligence opportunities.

Open-source intelligence (OSINT) practitioners should leverage online communities, forums, and conferences to network and exchange ideas with peers. Participating in discussions and sharing experiences can provide valuable perspectives and lead to innovative intelligence gathering approaches.

Another effective strategy is to conduct regular reviews and assessments of intelligence gathering processes. Professionals should analyze past intelligence projects to identify areas for improvement, such as data sources, collection methods, and analysis techniques. Command-line tools like "awk" and "sed" can be used to manipulate and process data for analysis.

Incorporating feedback loops into intelligence gathering processes is essential. Collecting feedback from stakeholders, clients, and end-users helps intelligence professionals understand their needs and expectations. Command-line tools like "tee" can be used to capture command output for documentation and analysis.

Intelligence professionals should also stay informed about changes in legal and ethical standards related to intelligence gathering. Compliance with laws and regulations is crucial to maintaining trust and credibility. Staying updated on relevant legislation and guidelines is vital for continuous improvement.

Another important strategy is to diversify data sources. Relying on a single source for intelligence gathering can be risky, as it may lead to biased or incomplete information. Command-line tools like "wget" and "curl" can be used to retrieve data from various online sources.

Additionally, intelligence professionals should develop critical thinking skills to assess the credibility and reliability of information sources. Command-line tools like "sort" and "uniq" can be employed to identify patterns and inconsistencies in data.

Continuous improvement in intelligence gathering also involves adapting to emerging threats and challenges. Intelligence professionals should anticipate evolving threat landscapes and be prepared to adjust their strategies accordingly. Command-line tools like "diff" can be used to compare and identify changes in datasets over time.

Furthermore, organizations should invest in research and development efforts to explore innovative intelligence gathering techniques and technologies. Experimenting with new tools and approaches can lead to breakthroughs in data collection and analysis. Command-line tools like "git" can be used for version control and collaboration on research projects.

In summary, strategies for continuous improvement in intelligence gathering encompass a range of approaches and practices. These strategies include fostering a culture of learning, embracing technology advancements, automating processes, establishing data management practices, fostering collaboration, conducting regular reviews and assessments, incorporating feedback loops, staying informed about legal and ethical standards, diversifying data sources, developing critical thinking skills, adapting to emerging threats, and investing in research and development.

By implementing these strategies, intelligence professionals and organizations can enhance their intelligence gathering capabilities, adapt to changing landscapes, and ultimately make more informed decisions to protect their interests and security.

BOOK 3
AIRCRAFT-NG UNLEASHED
ADVANCED CLI MASTERY IN OSINT INVESTIGATIONS

ROB BOTWRIGHT

Chapter 1: Introduction to Aircrack-ng and OSINT

Understanding wireless security and OSINT (Open Source Intelligence) is essential in today's interconnected world, where wireless networks play a pivotal role in our daily lives.

Wireless networks, including Wi-Fi and cellular networks, have become ubiquitous, providing convenient connectivity for both individuals and organizations. However, the convenience of wireless technology also introduces security risks that must be comprehensively understood and managed.

One fundamental aspect of wireless security is the protection of data transmitted over wireless networks. Encryption protocols like WEP, WPA, and WPA2/WPA3 are used to secure wireless communications, ensuring that data remains confidential and protected from eavesdropping. Understanding these encryption protocols and their vulnerabilities is crucial for assessing wireless security.

Moreover, OSINT professionals should be familiar with the tools and techniques employed by malicious actors to compromise wireless networks. Tools like "Aircrack-ng" and "Wireshark" can be used to capture and analyze wireless network traffic, potentially revealing vulnerabilities or unauthorized access.

Additionally, understanding the concept of Wi-Fi access points (APs) and their configuration is vital for wireless security. OSINT professionals should know how to identify rogue APs that may be used for malicious purposes, such as setting up fake hotspots to intercept data or conduct man-in-the-middle attacks.

Furthermore, knowledge of wireless network protocols and authentication methods is crucial. OSINT practitioners should be aware of common authentication mechanisms like WPA-PSK (Pre-Shared Key) and WPA-Enterprise, as well as the vulnerabilities associated with each method.

Understanding the wireless spectrum and frequency bands is also essential for wireless security. Different frequency bands, such as 2.4 GHz and 5 GHz, are used for Wi-Fi, and OSINT professionals should be aware of the advantages and limitations of each. Moreover, understanding the range and coverage of wireless networks can help assess potential security risks.

In addition to understanding wireless security principles, OSINT professionals must be proficient in using command-line tools to assess and test the security of wireless networks. For example, "iwconfig" can be used to view wireless network interfaces and their configurations, while "airmon-ng" is employed to enable monitor mode for wireless network analysis.

Furthermore, OSINT practitioners should be familiar with command-line tools like "aireplay-ng" and "mdk3," which can be used to test the security of wireless networks by injecting traffic, de-authenticating clients, and performing denial-of-service attacks.

Understanding the concept of wireless security standards and best practices is crucial. OSINT professionals should stay informed about industry standards and recommendations for securing wireless networks. Command-line tools like "nmcli" and "wpa_cli" can be used to configure and manage wireless network settings on Linux-based systems.

In addition to securing wireless networks, OSINT professionals should also consider the security of wireless devices. Understanding the vulnerabilities and risks associated with wireless devices like smartphones, tablets, and IoT (Internet of Things) devices is essential.

Moreover, knowledge of wireless intrusion detection and prevention systems (IDS/IPS) is valuable. These systems can help monitor and protect wireless networks from unauthorized access and attacks. Understanding the command-line tools used for managing IDS/IPS configurations can be beneficial for wireless security assessments.

Furthermore, OSINT professionals should be aware of the challenges posed by open Wi-Fi networks, such as public hotspots. These networks are often unencrypted and can be targets for attackers looking to intercept data. Command-line tools like "tcpdump" can be used to capture and analyze network traffic on open Wi-Fi networks.

Understanding the concept of war-driving is also relevant in the context of wireless security and OSINT. War-driving involves scanning for and mapping wireless networks while driving or walking in urban areas. OSINT professionals should be familiar with the tools and techniques used for war-driving, including GPS mapping and data collection.

Moreover, knowledge of wireless security auditing and penetration testing is crucial. OSINT professionals should understand how to use command-line tools like "Kismet" and "Reaver" to assess the security of wireless networks, identify vulnerabilities, and recommend mitigation strategies.

Additionally, OSINT professionals should be aware of the legal and ethical considerations related to wireless security assessments. Conducting unauthorized penetration testing or attempting to compromise wireless networks without proper authorization can have legal consequences.

In summary, understanding wireless security and OSINT is essential for individuals and organizations seeking to protect their wireless networks and data. OSINT professionals should have a solid grasp of wireless encryption protocols, tools and techniques for wireless network analysis, Wi-Fi access points, authentication methods, wireless spectrum, and best practices for securing wireless networks and devices.

Command-line tools play a significant role in assessing and testing wireless security, and proficiency in using these tools is valuable for OSINT practitioners. Moreover, staying informed about industry standards, wireless intrusion detection systems, open Wi-Fi networks, war-driving, security auditing, and legal and ethical considerations is essential for a comprehensive understanding of wireless security and OSINT.

Exploring the role of Aircrack-ng in OSINT (Open Source Intelligence) investigations unveils a powerful set of tools and techniques for assessing wireless security and conducting network reconnaissance. Aircrack-ng is a suite of command-line utilities designed for capturing, analyzing, and cracking Wi-Fi network encryption, making it a valuable asset in the OSINT practitioner's toolkit. One of the primary functions of Aircrack-ng is to capture wireless network traffic, which is crucial for assessing the security of Wi-Fi networks. The "airmon-ng" command is used to enable monitor mode on a wireless network interface, allowing it to capture packets from nearby Wi-Fi networks.

In addition to capturing traffic, Aircrack-ng provides tools for analyzing and decrypting encrypted network communications. The "aircrack-ng" command is specifically used for cracking WEP (Wired Equivalent Privacy) and WPA/WPA2 (Wi-Fi Protected Access) encryption keys, which are commonly used to secure wireless networks.

Aircrack-ng supports the use of external wordlists and dictionaries to aid in password cracking. OSINT professionals can employ command-line tools like "crunch" to generate custom wordlists tailored to the target network, increasing the chances of successful password recovery.

Moreover, Aircrack-ng includes tools for capturing handshakes exchanged between clients and access points during the authentication process. These handshakes can be later used for offline password cracking attempts. The "airodump-ng" command is used to capture handshakes and collect information about nearby Wi-Fi networks.

Understanding the command-line syntax and options for each Aircrack-ng tool is essential for OSINT professionals. The suite includes comprehensive documentation accessible through the "man" command, enabling users to access detailed information on command usage and parameters.

Furthermore, Aircrack-ng allows OSINT practitioners to perform Wi-Fi deauthentication attacks, also known as deauth attacks, using the "aireplay-ng" command. These attacks disrupt the connection between a client device and an access point, potentially forcing the client to reauthenticate and providing an opportunity to capture the handshake.

In OSINT investigations, Aircrack-ng can be used to assess the security of Wi-Fi networks within a target location. OSINT professionals can employ the suite to identify vulnerabilities in network encryption, test the strength of passwords, and determine the effectiveness of security measures.

Additionally, Aircrack-ng provides support for analyzing packet captures in standard PCAP (Packet Capture) format. OSINT practitioners can use tools like "tcpdump" to capture network traffic, and then analyze the captured data with Aircrack-ng utilities to gain insights into network activities and potential security weaknesses.

Understanding the concepts of Wi-Fi security standards, such as WEP, WPA, and WPA2/WPA3, is essential when using Aircrack-ng in OSINT investigations. These standards dictate the encryption methods and authentication mechanisms used by wireless networks, and OSINT professionals should be well-versed in their strengths and vulnerabilities.

Furthermore, Aircrack-ng supports the use of GPU acceleration for faster password cracking. OSINT practitioners with access to powerful graphics processing units can leverage this feature to significantly speed up the cracking process.

When conducting OSINT investigations involving Wi-Fi networks, OSINT professionals should always ensure that they have the appropriate authorization to assess network security. Unauthorized access to or testing of Wi-Fi networks may be illegal and can result in legal consequences.

In addition to assessing the security of Wi-Fi networks, Aircrack-ng can be a valuable tool for network reconnaissance in OSINT investigations. OSINT professionals can use Aircrack-ng to discover nearby Wi-Fi networks, collect information about their SSIDs (Service Set Identifiers), BSSIDs (Basic Service Set Identifiers), and channels, and identify potential targets for further investigation.

Furthermore, Aircrack-ng can assist in identifying hidden or non-broadcasted SSIDs, a technique commonly used by network administrators to enhance security. The suite's "airodump-ng" command can be used to scan for hidden SSIDs and gather information about the networks.

In OSINT investigations, Aircrack-ng can be used in conjunction with other tools and techniques to assess the security posture of target organizations or individuals. OSINT practitioners should consider incorporating the suite into their broader OSINT toolset to enhance their capabilities in network reconnaissance and wireless security assessment.

In summary, Aircrack-ng plays a significant role in OSINT investigations by providing a suite of command-line utilities for capturing, analyzing, and cracking Wi-Fi network encryption. OSINT professionals can leverage Aircrack-ng to assess the security of wireless networks, capture handshakes, perform deauthentication attacks, analyze packet captures, and conduct network reconnaissance.

Understanding the command-line syntax, options, and best practices for using Aircrack-ng is essential for OSINT practitioners seeking to enhance their wireless security assessment capabilities. However, it is essential to conduct such assessments within the bounds of legal and ethical considerations, obtaining proper authorization before engaging in any network security testing.

Chapter 2: Setting Up Your Aircrack-ng CLI Environment

Installing and configuring Aircrack-ng CLI (Command-Line Interface) is a critical step for OSINT (Open Source Intelligence) professionals who wish to leverage its powerful wireless security assessment capabilities.

Before diving into the installation process, it's essential to ensure that you are using a compatible operating system. Aircrack-ng is primarily designed for Unix-like operating systems, including Linux and macOS, and it may not be readily available for Windows. However, you can install it on Windows using tools like Windows Subsystem for Linux (WSL) or Cygwin.

For Linux-based systems, the installation of Aircrack-ng is relatively straightforward, thanks to package managers like APT (Advanced Package Tool) on Debian-based distributions (e.g., Ubuntu) and YUM (Yellowdog Updater Modified) on Red Hat-based distributions (e.g., Fedora).

To install Aircrack-ng on Ubuntu or Debian, you can use the following command:

arduinoCopy code

```
sudo apt-get install aircrack-ng
```

On Fedora or Red Hat-based systems, you can use the following command with YUM:

Copy code

```
sudo yum install aircrack-ng
```

Once you have successfully installed Aircrack-ng, you can verify the installation by running the following command:

cssCopy code

```
aircrack-ng --version
```

This command should display the version information of Aircrack-ng, confirming that the installation was successful.

Configuring Aircrack-ng CLI involves understanding its command-line options and preparing your system for wireless network assessment. Aircrack-ng provides a wide range of command-line tools, each with its specific functionality.

To view the available command-line options and help information for Aircrack-ng tools, you can use the "man" command followed by the tool's name. For example, to view the manual for "aircrack-ng," you can run:

Copy code

```
man aircrack-ng
```

This will provide detailed information about the usage, options, and syntax of the "aircrack-ng" command.

Before using Aircrack-ng CLI for wireless security assessments, it's crucial to have a compatible wireless network adapter that supports monitor mode and packet injection. Many built-in Wi-Fi adapters on laptops may not fully support these features, so it's often recommended to use an external USB wireless adapter known for its compatibility with Aircrack-ng.

To set your wireless network adapter to monitor mode, you can use the "airmon-ng" command. For example, if your wireless adapter is named "wlan0," you can run the following command to enable monitor mode:

sqlCopy code

```
sudo airmon-ng start wlan0
```

This command will create a new interface called "mon0" or similar, which is in monitor mode and ready for packet capturing and analysis.

Additionally, Aircrack-ng may require the installation of specific wireless drivers and firmware to ensure proper functionality. The package manager on your Linux distribution can often handle these dependencies automatically during installation.

Once your wireless network adapter is in monitor mode, you can use Aircrack-ng tools like "airodump-ng" to scan for nearby Wi-Fi networks and gather information about them. The "airodump-ng" command allows you to view details such as SSIDs, BSSIDs, channels, encryption types, and more.

For example, to scan for nearby networks on the "mon0" interface, you can run:

Copy code

```
sudo airodump-ng mon0
```

This command will display a list of detected wireless networks along with their essential information.

To perform more advanced tasks, such as capturing handshakes for password cracking or conducting deauthentication attacks, you'll need to familiarize yourself with the specific commands and options of the Aircrack-ng tools. These actions require a deeper understanding of wireless security principles and ethical considerations.

In summary, installing and configuring Aircrack-ng CLI is a crucial step for OSINT professionals looking to assess the security of wireless networks. It involves selecting a compatible operating system, installing Aircrack-ng using the package manager, and configuring a wireless network adapter for monitor mode.

Understanding the command-line options of Aircrack-ng tools, verifying the installation, and preparing your system for wireless security assessments are essential aspects of this process. However, it's vital to approach wireless security assessments with the appropriate knowledge, authorization, and ethical considerations to ensure responsible and lawful usage of these tools.

Navigating the Aircrack-ng Command Line Interface (CLI) is a fundamental skill for OSINT (Open Source Intelligence) professionals seeking to assess and secure wireless networks effectively. The Aircrack-ng suite provides a versatile set of CLI tools designed to capture, analyze, and manipulate Wi-Fi network data.

Before delving into the specific commands and functionalities of Aircrack-ng, it's crucial to understand the basic structure of its CLI interface. Aircrack-ng follows a standard command syntax, where each command is followed by options and arguments.

Typically, Aircrack-ng commands start with the name of the tool, such as "airmon-ng," "airodump-ng," or "aireplay-ng," followed by various options that modify the tool's behavior. These options are often preceded by a hyphen or double hyphen and are used to specify settings or parameters.

For example, the "airodump-ng" command, used for capturing Wi-Fi traffic and monitoring nearby networks, can be executed with various options, such as specifying the wireless interface to use, setting the channel to monitor, and specifying an output file for captured data.

Here is a basic example of the "airodump-ng" command with some common options:

cssCopy code

```
airodump-ng --interface wlan0mon --channel 6 --write
capturefile
```
In this example, "--interface" specifies the wireless interface to use (in monitor mode), "--channel" sets the channel to monitor, and "--write" specifies the name of the capture file to save the captured data.

To explore the capabilities of Aircrack-ng's CLI further, OSINT professionals can refer to the comprehensive documentation and manual pages provided with the suite. By running the "man" command followed by the name of a specific Aircrack-ng tool, users can access detailed information about the tool's usage, available options, and syntax.

For instance, to view the manual for "airodump-ng," one can execute the following command:

Copy code

```
man airodump-ng
```

This will display a detailed manual page with explanations of each option and examples of command usage.

A key aspect of navigating the Aircrack-ng CLI is understanding the various tools available within the suite and their respective purposes. Each tool serves a specific function in the context of wireless network assessment and security.

One of the essential Aircrack-ng tools is "airodump-ng," which is used for network discovery and packet capturing. It allows OSINT professionals to identify nearby Wi-Fi networks, view information about their SSIDs, BSSIDs, channels, and client devices, and capture network traffic for further analysis.

To navigate and interact with the "airodump-ng" interface effectively, users should familiarize themselves with its structure. The tool displays a list of detected Wi-Fi networks, updating in real-time as new networks appear or existing ones disappear. OSINT practitioners can use keyboard shortcuts to control the tool's behavior, such as pressing "Ctrl+C" to stop capturing and save data.

Another crucial Aircrack-ng tool is "aireplay-ng," which specializes in packet injection and manipulation. OSINT professionals can use "aireplay-ng" to perform deauthentication attacks, reassociation attacks, and other packet-level activities to assess network security and capture handshakes for password cracking.

Navigating the "aireplay-ng" interface involves understanding the different attack modes and options available. For example, the tool offers modes like "deauth," "fakeauth," and "arpreplay," each designed for specific types of attacks. OSINT practitioners should review the tool's manual and experiment in a controlled environment to gain proficiency.

Furthermore, Aircrack-ng includes the "aircrack-ng" tool, which is used for WEP and WPA/WPA2 handshake capture and password cracking. While navigating the "aircrack-ng" CLI interface, users can specify the capture file containing handshakes and select a dictionary or wordlist for password attempts.

Navigating the "aircrack-ng" tool effectively requires understanding the syntax for initiating password cracking attempts and monitoring progress. OSINT professionals should also be aware of the importance of having a high-quality wordlist for successful password recovery.

In addition to the primary Aircrack-ng tools mentioned, the suite offers utilities like "airmon-ng" for managing monitor mode interfaces, "airodump-ng-oui-update" for updating OUI (Organizationally Unique Identifier) databases, and "ivstools" for working with IVs (Initialization Vectors).

As OSINT professionals navigate the Aircrack-ng CLI, they should always keep ethical considerations and legal implications in mind. Using Aircrack-ng for unauthorized network assessments or malicious purposes is against the law in many jurisdictions and can lead to legal consequences.

Moreover, ethical OSINT practitioners should obtain proper authorization before engaging in wireless security assessments and follow responsible disclosure practices when identifying vulnerabilities in Wi-Fi networks. The use of Aircrack-ng and similar tools should be aligned with a commitment to security and privacy, promoting the responsible and ethical use of wireless network assessment tools.

In summary, navigating the Aircrack-ng Command Line Interface is essential for OSINT professionals aiming to assess and secure wireless networks effectively. Understanding the structure of Aircrack-ng commands, referencing the documentation and manual pages, and familiarizing oneself with the suite's tools and their purposes are key elements of successful navigation.

Furthermore, ethical considerations and compliance with legal requirements should always be at the forefront of OSINT practitioners' minds when conducting wireless network assessments using Aircrack-ng or similar tools. Responsible and lawful usage is paramount to maintaining ethical integrity and trust in the field of OSINT.

Chapter 3: Capturing and Analyzing Wireless Packets

Capturing wireless data traffic is a fundamental task in the realm of network analysis and security assessment, and it plays a vital role in Open Source Intelligence (OSINT) investigations where understanding network activities is crucial.

One of the primary tools for capturing wireless data traffic is Airodump-ng, a versatile command-line utility that is part of the Aircrack-ng suite.

To initiate wireless data traffic capture with Airodump-ng, you need to specify the wireless network interface you want to use for monitoring.

The "airodump-ng" command typically takes the following form:

csharpCopy code

```
airodump-ng -- interface < interface >
```

Here, **<interface>** represents the name of your wireless network interface, which should be set to monitor mode before using Airodump-ng.

Monitor mode enables your wireless adapter to capture all wireless frames and packets in the air, not just those intended for your device.

To put your wireless adapter into monitor mode, you can use the "airmon-ng" command:

csharpCopy code

```
airmon-ng start < interface >
```

This command will create a new virtual interface, usually named something like "mon0," which will be in monitor mode and ready for capturing wireless data traffic.

Once your interface is in monitor mode, you can run the "airodump-ng" command with additional options to specify the channel, capture file, and other parameters.

For example, to capture data traffic on channel 6 and save it to a file called "capturefile," you can use the following command:

cssCopy code

```
airodump-ng --channel 6 --write capturefile mon0
```

This command tells Airodump-ng to listen on channel 6 and write the captured data to a file named "capturefile."

Airodump-ng will display a table showing nearby wireless networks, including their SSIDs (Service Set Identifiers), BSSIDs (Basic Service Set Identifiers), power levels, and data traffic activity.

The "Data" column in the table indicates the amount of data traffic being exchanged on each network. This is a valuable metric for OSINT professionals looking to identify active networks or specific devices of interest.

By monitoring the "Data" column, OSINT practitioners can gain insights into which networks are actively in use, potentially revealing targets for further investigation.

Additionally, Airodump-ng provides the capability to capture handshake packets, which are essential for cracking WPA/WPA2 Wi-Fi passwords.

To capture a handshake, OSINT professionals can use the "airodump-ng" command in a similar manner but with a specific target network in mind:

cssCopy code

```
airodump-ng --channel 6 --bssid <target_BSSID> --write capturefile mon0
```

In this command, **<target_BSSID>** represents the BSSID of the network you want to target.

172

Airodump-ng will focus its capture efforts on the specified network, attempting to collect the handshake packets exchanged between devices and the access point during the authentication process.

Capturing handshake packets is a critical step in OSINT investigations involving Wi-Fi networks, as these packets are necessary for offline password cracking.

Furthermore, OSINT professionals can use the "aireplay-ng" tool, also part of the Aircrack-ng suite, to inject additional traffic into the network, potentially increasing the chances of capturing handshake packets.

However, it's important to note that capturing wireless data traffic should always be conducted within the bounds of legal and ethical considerations.

Unauthorized monitoring of wireless networks, especially those belonging to others, may violate privacy and legal regulations in many jurisdictions.

OSINT practitioners must obtain proper authorization to conduct network assessments and data traffic capture, ensuring that their actions align with ethical standards and legal requirements.

In summary, capturing wireless data traffic using tools like Airodump-ng is a crucial task in OSINT investigations and network security assessments.

By leveraging the capabilities of Airodump-ng, OSINT professionals can monitor nearby networks, identify active devices, and capture handshake packets for further analysis.

However, ethical and legal considerations should always guide the actions of OSINT practitioners when conducting wireless data traffic capture, promoting responsible and lawful usage of these tools in the pursuit of open source intelligence.

Analyzing packet data for insights is a critical component of network analysis and Open Source Intelligence (OSINT) investigations, as it allows professionals to extract valuable information from the captured network traffic.
One of the key tools for analyzing packet data is Wireshark, a powerful and versatile packet capture and analysis tool that provides a graphical user interface (GUI) for in-depth network traffic inspection.
Wireshark is particularly useful in OSINT investigations because it enables analysts to dissect network packets, extract data, and uncover patterns and anomalies.
To begin analyzing packet data with Wireshark, you first need to capture the network traffic of interest.
Wireshark can capture packets from various sources, including live network interfaces, previously saved capture files, or even remote systems using technologies like SSH (Secure Shell) or RPCAP (Remote Packet Capture Protocol).
To capture live network traffic, you can use the "Capture Options" dialog in Wireshark's interface.
This dialog allows you to select the specific network interface you want to capture packets from and configure various capture settings, such as packet filters, promiscuous mode, and capture file location.
Once you've configured the capture options, you can start the packet capture process by clicking the "Start" button.
Wireshark will begin capturing packets from the selected network interface, displaying them in real-time in its main window.

As packets are captured, Wireshark provides detailed information about each packet, including source and destination addresses, protocols used, and packet lengths. One of the strengths of Wireshark is its ability to dissect and decode various network protocols, making it possible to analyze the contents of network traffic at a granular level.

OSINT professionals can use Wireshark's protocol dissectors to inspect the data within each packet, even for encrypted protocols like HTTPS (Hypertext Transfer Protocol Secure).

Wireshark's ability to dissect encrypted traffic depends on whether the analyst has access to the encryption keys or can decrypt the traffic through other means.

For encrypted protocols like HTTPS, Wireshark may not be able to provide the contents of the encrypted data, but it can still provide valuable metadata and insights, such as the timing and size of encrypted requests.

Beyond simply capturing and inspecting packets, Wireshark also offers powerful filtering and analysis capabilities.

Using display filters, OSINT analysts can focus on specific types of packets or traffic patterns, allowing them to extract meaningful insights from large packet captures.

For example, you can use display filters to isolate packets that match specific criteria, such as packets originating from or destined for a particular IP address, packets using a particular protocol, or packets with specific keywords in their payload.

Wireshark also provides statistical analysis tools that can help OSINT professionals gain insights into network behavior.

For instance, you can use Wireshark's "Statistics" menu to generate various network statistics, including packet and byte counts, conversation summaries, and protocol hierarchy statistics.

These statistics can reveal patterns, anomalies, or trends within the captured network traffic, which may be relevant to an OSINT investigation.

Furthermore, Wireshark allows you to export packet data or analysis results for further processing or sharing.

You can save captured packets in various file formats, including the commonly used PCAP (Packet Capture) format, which is compatible with many other network analysis tools.

Additionally, Wireshark provides the ability to export summary statistics, conversations, or specific packets in various formats, making it easy to collaborate with other analysts or include findings in reports.

While Wireshark is a powerful tool for analyzing packet data, it's essential to approach network packet analysis with ethical and legal considerations in mind.

Capturing network traffic without proper authorization or monitoring networks that do not belong to you can have legal and ethical implications.

OSINT professionals must ensure that their actions align with ethical standards and legal requirements when conducting packet data analysis, especially when dealing with sensitive or private information.

In summary, analyzing packet data for insights is a crucial aspect of network analysis and OSINT investigations, and Wireshark is a valuable tool for this purpose.

With its ability to capture, dissect, and analyze network traffic, Wireshark empowers OSINT professionals to extract valuable information, uncover patterns, and gain insights into network behavior.

However, responsible and ethical usage of Wireshark is paramount, and professionals should always obtain proper authorization and adhere to legal requirements when conducting packet data analysis in the context of OSINT investigations.

Chapter 4: Cracking WEP and WPA/WPA2 Encryption

Cracking WEP (Wired Equivalent Privacy) encryption using Aircrack-ng is a classic and essential skill for network security professionals and ethical hackers.

Before diving into the specifics of cracking WEP encryption, it's crucial to understand the vulnerabilities inherent in this outdated security protocol.

WEP was the first encryption protocol used to secure Wi-Fi networks, but it has long been considered weak and insecure due to several critical flaws.

One of the main vulnerabilities of WEP is its reliance on a static encryption key, which means that the same encryption key is used for all data packets transmitted over the network.

This static key makes it susceptible to attacks because once an attacker captures enough encrypted packets, they can apply various techniques to recover the key.

Aircrack-ng is a powerful toolset designed to exploit these weaknesses and recover WEP encryption keys.

The process of cracking WEP encryption with Aircrack-ng typically involves capturing enough WEP-encrypted packets from the target network.

To capture the necessary packets, you can use the "airodump-ng" tool, which is part of the Aircrack-ng suite.

The "airodump-ng" command allows you to scan for nearby Wi-Fi networks and collect information about them, including the target network's BSSID (Basic Service Set Identifier), channel, and data traffic activity.

For example, you can use the following command to scan for networks and capture data packets from a specific target network:

phpCopy code

```
airodump-ng --bssid <target_BSSID> --channel <channel> --write <capture_file> <interface>
```

In this command, **<target_BSSID>** represents the BSSID of the target network, **<channel>** is the channel on which the target network operates, **<capture_file>** is the name of the file to save the captured packets, and **<interface>** is the name of your wireless network interface in monitor mode.

Once you have collected a sufficient number of WEP-encrypted packets, you can proceed with the key recovery process using Aircrack-ng.

The key recovery process involves using Aircrack-ng's "aircrack-ng" command with the captured packets as input:

phpCopy code

```
aircrack-ng -a 1 -b <target_BSSID> -e <ESSID> <capture_file>
```

In this command, **-a 1** specifies that you are targeting WEP encryption, **-b <target_BSSID>** specifies the BSSID of the target network, **-e <ESSID>** specifies the ESSID (Extended Service Set Identifier) or SSID of the target network (optional but helpful for identifying the network), and **<capture_file>** is the name of the file containing the captured packets.

Aircrack-ng will analyze the captured packets and attempt to recover the WEP encryption key used by the target network.

The key recovery process relies on statistical analysis and computational techniques to find the correct key.

It may take some time, depending on the quality and quantity of captured packets and the complexity of the WEP key.

Once Aircrack-ng successfully recovers the WEP key, it will display the key in hexadecimal format, which can then be used to decrypt the network's traffic.

It's important to note that cracking WEP encryption is considered a security research activity and should only be performed on networks for which you have explicit authorization.

Cracking WEP encryption on networks you do not own or have permission to assess is illegal and unethical.

Moreover, WEP encryption is no longer considered secure, and most modern Wi-Fi networks use more robust encryption protocols like WPA2 or WPA3.

In practical security assessments, professionals should focus on testing the security of networks with strong encryption methods rather than wasting time on WEP-protected networks, as WEP has been deprecated for well-founded security reasons.

In summary, cracking WEP encryption with Aircrack-ng is a valuable skill for understanding the vulnerabilities of outdated security protocols.

It involves capturing enough encrypted packets from a target network and then using Aircrack-ng to recover the WEP key.

However, ethical considerations and legal requirements must guide the use of this technique, and professionals should prioritize assessing networks with stronger encryption standards in real-world security assessments.

Breaking WPA (Wi-Fi Protected Access) and WPA2 (Wi-Fi Protected Access 2) security using Aircrack-ng is a challenging but essential skill for penetration testers and security professionals.

Before delving into the specifics of breaking WPA/WPA2 security, it's crucial to understand the motivation behind these attempts.

Ethical hacking and security assessments often involve testing the security of Wi-Fi networks to identify vulnerabilities and weaknesses that could be exploited by malicious actors.

WPA and WPA2 are encryption protocols used to protect wireless networks, and breaking their security can help identify weak or improperly configured networks.

However, it's important to note that attempting to break the security of a Wi-Fi network without explicit authorization is illegal and unethical.

Only conduct security assessments on networks for which you have obtained proper permission.

WPA and WPA2 both use a passphrase (pre-shared key or PSK) to secure the network.

To break the security, you need to recover this passphrase through a process called a dictionary or brute-force attack.

Aircrack-ng provides a suite of tools that can assist in this process.

The first step in attempting to break WPA/WPA2 security is to capture the WPA handshake, which occurs when a device authenticates with the network.

To capture the WPA handshake, you can use the "airodump-ng" tool from the Aircrack-ng suite.

The "airodump-ng" command allows you to scan for nearby Wi-Fi networks, collect information about them, and capture the handshake when a device connects.

For example, you can use the following command to capture the handshake from a target network:

phpCopy code

airodump-ng --bssid <target_BSSID> --channel <channel> --write <capture_file> <interface>

In this command, **<target_BSSID>** represents the BSSID of the target network, **<channel>** is the channel on which the target network operates, **<capture_file>** is the name of the file to save the captured handshake, and **<interface>** is the name of your wireless network interface in monitor mode.

Once you've successfully captured the WPA handshake, you can proceed with the passphrase recovery process using Aircrack-ng.

Aircrack-ng includes a tool called "aircrack-ng" that can attempt to recover the passphrase from the captured handshake.

The basic syntax for using "aircrack-ng" is as follows:

phpCopy code

aircrack-ng -a 2 -b <target_BSSID> -w <wordlist_file> <capture_file>

In this command, **-a 2** specifies that you are targeting WPA/WPA2 encryption, **-b <target_BSSID>** specifies the BSSID of the target network, **-w <wordlist_file>** specifies the path to a wordlist file containing possible passphrases, and **<capture_file>** is the name of the file containing the captured handshake.

Aircrack-ng will systematically try each passphrase from the wordlist against the captured handshake until it finds the correct one or exhausts the list. The success of this attack depends on the strength of the passphrase and the quality of the wordlist. If the target network is using a weak or common passphrase, it may be vulnerable to this type of attack. However, strong and complex passphrases are more resistant to dictionary and brute-force attacks.

To enhance your chances of success, you can use high-quality wordlists that include a wide range of possible passphrases, including common words, phrases, and variations.

It's essential to emphasize that breaking WPA/WPA2 security should only be performed on networks for which you have explicit authorization.

Unethical or unauthorized attempts to crack Wi-Fi encryption are illegal and can lead to serious consequences.

Furthermore, modern Wi-Fi networks should use WPA3 encryption, which is significantly more secure than WPA and WPA2.

In summary, breaking WPA/WPA2 security with Aircrack-ng is a skill that security professionals may use to assess the security of Wi-Fi networks.

It involves capturing the WPA handshake and attempting to recover the passphrase using dictionary or brute-force attacks.

However, ethical considerations and legal requirements should always guide the use of these techniques, and professionals should prioritize assessing networks with stronger encryption standards in real-world security assessments.

Chapter 5: Advanced Wi-Fi Attacks and Techniques

Exploring advanced Wi-Fi attack strategies is a crucial aspect of cybersecurity and ethical hacking, as it helps professionals understand and defend against potential threats to wireless networks.

These advanced strategies build upon the foundational knowledge of Wi-Fi security and expand the toolkit for assessing and mitigating risks.

One advanced attack strategy involves the use of rogue access points, which are unauthorized Wi-Fi access points set up to mimic legitimate networks.

These rogue access points can be used by attackers to intercept data or launch man-in-the-middle attacks.

To detect rogue access points, security professionals can utilize tools like Kismet or Wireshark to monitor nearby networks and identify unauthorized devices.

Another advanced Wi-Fi attack strategy is the creation of evil twin networks, which are rogue access points that mimic legitimate networks to trick users into connecting.

Attackers can use evil twins to capture sensitive information, such as login credentials, by intercepting data transmitted through the rogue access point.

Defending against evil twin attacks requires network administrators to implement strong authentication methods and educate users about the risks of connecting to unknown networks.

MAC (Media Access Control) address spoofing is another advanced technique used by attackers to bypass MAC address filtering on wireless networks.

MAC address filtering is a security measure that allows or denies access to a network based on the MAC addresses of devices.

Attackers can use tools like Macchanger to spoof their device's MAC address and gain unauthorized access to the network.

To counter MAC address spoofing, network administrators should implement additional security measures, such as WPA3 encryption and strong authentication protocols.

WPS (Wi-Fi Protected Setup) attacks represent another advanced Wi-Fi attack strategy.

WPS is a feature that simplifies the process of connecting devices to a Wi-Fi network by using a PIN or a push-button method.

However, WPS can also be exploited by attackers to gain unauthorized access to the network.

Tools like Reaver and Bully automate WPS attacks by attempting to guess the WPS PIN.

To defend against WPS attacks, it is recommended to disable WPS on the network router or access point.

Deauthentication attacks, also known as deauth attacks or deauthentications, are advanced techniques used to disrupt Wi-Fi connections.

These attacks send deauthentication frames to connected devices, causing them to disconnect from the network.

Attackers can use deauth attacks to force users to reconnect, potentially revealing their Wi-Fi credentials.

To protect against deauth attacks, network administrators can monitor for unusual activity and implement intrusion detection systems (IDS) or intrusion prevention systems (IPS).

Packet injection attacks are another advanced Wi-Fi attack strategy that involves sending custom-crafted packets to exploit vulnerabilities in Wi-Fi drivers or protocols.

These attacks can be used to compromise network security, intercept traffic, or launch other malicious activities.

Tools like Aircrack-ng and Scapy enable security professionals to perform packet injection attacks for testing and assessment purposes.

To mitigate the risks of packet injection attacks, it is essential to keep Wi-Fi drivers and firmware up to date and apply security patches promptly.

Man-in-the-middle (MitM) attacks on Wi-Fi networks are advanced techniques where an attacker intercepts and possibly alters communications between two parties.

MitM attacks can be used to eavesdrop on sensitive data or inject malicious content into network traffic.

Defending against MitM attacks involves using secure protocols such as HTTPS, implementing certificate validation, and monitoring network traffic for unusual patterns.

Some advanced Wi-Fi attack strategies target specific vulnerabilities in network protocols or encryption methods.

For example, the KRACK (Key Reinstallation Attack) vulnerability exploited weaknesses in the WPA2 encryption protocol, allowing attackers to intercept and decrypt Wi-Fi traffic.

Network administrators and security professionals must stay informed about such vulnerabilities and apply patches and updates promptly to protect their networks.

While exploring advanced Wi-Fi attack strategies is essential for security professionals, it is equally important to act responsibly and ethically.

Unauthorized and malicious use of these techniques can lead to legal consequences and harm individuals or organizations.

Security professionals should only employ advanced Wi-Fi attack strategies within the boundaries of ethical hacking and with proper authorization.

In summary, advanced Wi-Fi attack strategies are essential components of ethical hacking and cybersecurity.

These techniques help security professionals identify and mitigate vulnerabilities in wireless networks, protecting against potential threats.

However, responsible and ethical use of these strategies is paramount, and professionals must always adhere to legal and ethical standards when conducting Wi-Fi assessments and testing network security.

Leveraging Aircrack-ng for advanced exploits is a critical skill for security professionals and ethical hackers aiming to assess and secure wireless networks.

Aircrack-ng is a versatile and powerful toolset designed specifically for assessing the security of Wi-Fi networks and exploiting vulnerabilities.

One of the advanced exploits that Aircrack-ng facilitates is the cracking of Wi-Fi encryption keys, such as WEP, WPA, and WPA2, to gain unauthorized access to a network.

To crack these encryption keys, security professionals can use Aircrack-ng's suite of tools, including airodump-ng for packet capture and aircrack-ng for key recovery.

The process involves capturing a sufficient number of data packets from the target network and then attempting to recover the encryption key.

Aircrack-ng supports both dictionary-based and brute-force attacks, making it a valuable asset for assessing the strength of Wi-Fi security.

Another advanced exploit involves the use of deauthentication attacks, where Aircrack-ng can send deauthentication frames to disconnect devices from a Wi-Fi network.

This technique can be used to disrupt network connections, potentially forcing users to reconnect and revealing Wi-Fi credentials.

Aircrack-ng's ability to inject packets into a network can also be leveraged for various exploits, such as ARP (Address Resolution Protocol) spoofing attacks.

ARP spoofing allows attackers to intercept and manipulate network traffic, leading to potential data interception and man-in-the-middle attacks.

Aircrack-ng's packet injection capabilities can automate and streamline the execution of these attacks for security assessments and testing.

Cracking WEP encryption is one of the fundamental exploits that Aircrack-ng enables.

WEP (Wired Equivalent Privacy) is an outdated and weak encryption protocol used to secure Wi-Fi networks.

Aircrack-ng provides tools like airodump-ng and aircrack-ng to capture WEP-encrypted packets and recover the encryption key.

This exploit serves as a valuable lesson in the vulnerabilities of obsolete encryption methods.

Another advanced exploit facilitated by Aircrack-ng involves the cracking of WPA (Wi-Fi Protected Access) and WPA2 encryption keys.

WPA and WPA2 are more secure than WEP but can still be vulnerable if weak passphrases are used.

Aircrack-ng allows security professionals to capture the WPA handshake and attempt to recover the passphrase using dictionary or brute-force attacks.

This exploit highlights the importance of strong and complex passphrases in Wi-Fi security.

Aircrack-ng also plays a significant role in testing the security of WPS (Wi-Fi Protected Setup), a feature that simplifies the process of connecting devices to a Wi-Fi network.

WPS attacks, including those using Aircrack-ng tools like Reaver and Bully, can expose vulnerabilities in networks that have WPS enabled.

Mitigating these vulnerabilities often requires disabling WPS on the network router or access point.

Packet injection attacks using Aircrack-ng tools like aireplay-ng allow security professionals to exploit weaknesses in Wi-Fi drivers or protocols.

These attacks can be used to compromise network security, intercept traffic, or launch other malicious activities.

The ability to inject packets into a network is a powerful feature for testing and assessing network vulnerabilities.

Aircrack-ng also supports the creation of evil twin networks, which are rogue access points that mimic legitimate networks to trick users into connecting.

This exploit can be used to intercept sensitive information, such as login credentials, by intercepting data transmitted through the rogue access point.

Defending against evil twin attacks requires network administrators to implement strong authentication methods and educate users about the risks of connecting to unknown networks.

Aircrack-ng can assist in the detection of rogue access points by monitoring nearby networks and identifying unauthorized devices.

MAC (Media Access Control) address spoofing is an advanced technique that can be used by attackers to bypass MAC address filtering on wireless networks.

MAC address filtering is a security measure that allows or denies access to a network based on the MAC addresses of devices.

Tools like Macchanger, which are compatible with Aircrack-ng, can spoof a device's MAC address to gain unauthorized access to the network.

To counter MAC address spoofing, network administrators should implement additional security measures, such as WPA3 encryption and strong authentication protocols.

Deauthentication attacks, also known as deauth attacks or deauthentications, are advanced techniques used to disrupt Wi-Fi connections.

These attacks send deauthentication frames to connected devices, causing them to disconnect from the network.

Attackers can use deauth attacks to force users to reconnect, potentially revealing their Wi-Fi credentials.

To protect against deauth attacks, network administrators can monitor for unusual activity and implement intrusion detection systems (IDS) or intrusion prevention systems (IPS).

Packet injection attacks are another advanced Wi-Fi exploit strategy enabled by Aircrack-ng.

These attacks involve sending custom-crafted packets to exploit vulnerabilities in Wi-Fi drivers or protocols.

Tools like Aircrack-ng and Scapy allow security professionals to perform packet injection attacks for testing and assessment purposes.

To mitigate the risks of packet injection attacks, it is essential to keep Wi-Fi drivers and firmware up to date and apply security patches promptly.

Man-in-the-middle (MitM) attacks on Wi-Fi networks are advanced techniques where an attacker intercepts and possibly alters communications between two parties.

MitM attacks can be used to eavesdrop on sensitive data or inject malicious content into network traffic.

Defending against MitM attacks involves using secure protocols such as HTTPS, implementing certificate validation, and monitoring network traffic for unusual patterns.

Some advanced Wi-Fi exploit strategies target specific vulnerabilities in network protocols or encryption methods.

For example, the KRACK (Key Reinstallation Attack) vulnerability exploited weaknesses in the WPA2 encryption protocol, allowing attackers to intercept and decrypt Wi-Fi traffic.

Network administrators and security professionals must stay informed about such vulnerabilities and apply patches and updates promptly to protect their networks.

While exploring advanced Wi-Fi exploit strategies is crucial for security professionals, responsible and ethical use of these techniques is paramount.

Unauthorized and malicious use of these techniques can lead to legal consequences and harm individuals or organizations.

Security professionals should only employ advanced Wi-Fi exploit strategies within the boundaries of ethical hacking and with proper authorization.

In summary, leveraging Aircrack-ng for advanced exploits is a valuable skill for security professionals and ethical hackers.

These exploits help assess and secure wireless networks by identifying vulnerabilities and weaknesses.

However, responsible and ethical use of these strategies is essential, and professionals must always adhere to legal and ethical standards when conducting Wi-Fi assessments and testing network security.

Chapter 6: Evading Detection and Hiding Your Tracks

Techniques for staying stealthy in wireless attacks are critical for ethical hackers and security professionals who want to conduct covert assessments of Wi-Fi networks.

Maintaining stealth is essential to avoid detection and maintain the integrity of security assessments.

One fundamental technique for staying stealthy in wireless attacks is the use of monitor mode.

Monitor mode allows a wireless network card to capture traffic without associating with any specific network.

By operating in monitor mode, attackers can passively monitor network traffic without alerting network administrators or raising suspicion.

To enable monitor mode on a wireless network card, you can use the "airmon-ng" command provided by Aircrack-ng:

csharpCopy code

```
airmon-ng start <interface>
```

Replace **<interface>** with the name of your wireless network card.

Another technique to maintain stealth is to limit the power of transmitted signals.

Reducing the transmission power of a wireless network card makes it less likely to be detected by network monitoring tools or other devices.

You can adjust the transmission power using the "iwconfig" command:

csharpCopy code

```
iwconfig <interface> txpower <value>
```

Replace **<interface>** with the name of your wireless network card and **<value>** with the desired transmission power level.

When conducting wireless attacks, it's crucial to be aware of nearby Wi-Fi networks and avoid suspicious naming conventions for your rogue access points.

Choosing inconspicuous network names (SSIDs) and disabling the broadcast of SSIDs can help maintain a low profile.

Additionally, security professionals should avoid using easily identifiable or default SSIDs that could raise suspicion.

Another stealthy technique is to use MAC address anonymization.

Attackers can change their device's MAC address to avoid being easily tracked or identified.

Tools like Macchanger or "ifconfig" can be used to change the MAC address:

```csharp
ifconfig <interface> hw ether <new_MAC_address>
```

Replace **<interface>** with your wireless network card and **<new_MAC_address>** with the desired MAC address.

For ethical hackers conducting penetration testing, it's crucial to maintain a low and controlled data transfer rate. High data transfer rates can attract attention and raise suspicion.

Adjusting the data transfer rate using the "iwconfig" command can help maintain a stealthy presence:

```csharp
iwconfig <interface> rate <desired_rate>
```

Replace **<interface>** with your wireless network card and **<desired_rate>** with the desired data transfer rate.

To minimize interference with legitimate Wi-Fi networks, ethical hackers should also select the appropriate channels for their rogue access points.

Choosing channels that are less congested and not used by nearby networks can help avoid detection.

You can use the "iwlist" command to view available channels:

csharpCopy code

```
iwlist <interface> channel
```

Replace **<interface>** with your wireless network card.

Another critical aspect of staying stealthy is the use of encryption and secure communication protocols.

Encrypting communication between devices and using secure authentication methods helps prevent eavesdropping and detection.

Additionally, ethical hackers should employ techniques such as VPNs (Virtual Private Networks) to tunnel their traffic through encrypted channels for added security.

To maintain stealth in wireless attacks, it's essential to minimize noise and network traffic generated by the attacker's device.

Unnecessary network activities or services running on the attacker's machine may attract attention and compromise the operation's stealthiness.

Close any unnecessary applications and services to reduce network noise and minimize the risk of detection.

When conducting wireless attacks, it's crucial to continuously monitor network traffic and adjust tactics accordingly.

Attackers should be prepared to adapt to changing network conditions and react to unexpected events that may reveal their presence.

Staying vigilant and responsive is key to maintaining stealth throughout the assessment.

In some cases, attackers may need to conduct reconnaissance before launching attacks to gather intelligence and assess the target network's vulnerabilities.

This reconnaissance phase should be conducted discreetly to avoid detection.

Ethical hackers can use tools like "airodump-ng" from the Aircrack-ng suite to passively scan and collect information about nearby Wi-Fi networks.

Stealthy reconnaissance involves observing network activity without sending any probing packets that may be detected.

Another technique for staying stealthy in wireless attacks is to spoof the MAC address of your rogue access point.

By spoofing the MAC address to match a legitimate network's MAC address, the attacker can reduce suspicion and make it harder for network administrators to differentiate between the rogue and genuine access points.

To spoof the MAC address, you can use tools like Macchanger or manually configure the MAC address in your access point's settings.

It's essential to choose a MAC address carefully, ensuring that it doesn't conflict with an existing network device.

To maintain a low profile, ethical hackers should avoid broadcasting their rogue access points widely.

Instead, they can use a directed beacon strategy, where the access point only responds to specific client requests.

This technique reduces the visibility of the rogue access point, making it less likely to be discovered by casual network scans.

Additionally, using stealthy beacon frames and keeping the SSID hidden can further minimize the risk of detection.

In summary, techniques for staying stealthy in wireless attacks are crucial for ethical hackers and security professionals.

These techniques involve using monitor mode, adjusting transmission power, choosing inconspicuous SSIDs, MAC address anonymization, controlling data transfer rates, selecting appropriate channels, encrypting communication, minimizing network noise, conducting discreet reconnaissance, spoofing MAC addresses, and employing directed beacon strategies.

By mastering these techniques and maintaining a low profile, ethical hackers can conduct covert assessments of Wi-Fi networks while minimizing the risk of detection and interference with legitimate networks.

Covering your tracks in OSINT investigations is a crucial aspect of maintaining the confidentiality and integrity of your work.

When conducting open-source intelligence (OSINT) research, you often gather sensitive information, and it's essential to protect both your identity and the sources of your data.

One fundamental principle of covering your tracks in OSINT investigations is to use anonymous or pseudonymous online personas.

By creating and using online personas that are not directly linked to your real identity, you can conduct research without exposing yourself.

This involves using different usernames, email addresses, and profiles for OSINT activities to prevent anyone from tracing the information back to you.

Using a VPN (Virtual Private Network) is another essential step in maintaining anonymity during OSINT investigations.

A VPN routes your internet traffic through encrypted tunnels, hiding your real IP address and location.

This makes it much more challenging for anyone to track your online activities or determine your physical whereabouts.

To use a VPN, you can sign up for a reputable VPN service and install their client software on your device.

Once connected to the VPN, your internet traffic will be securely routed through their servers.

It's also crucial to use Tor (The Onion Router) when conducting OSINT investigations that involve accessing websites or resources on the dark web or deep web.

Tor is a network of volunteer-run servers that provides a high level of anonymity by routing your traffic through multiple nodes, making it difficult for anyone to trace your online activities.

You can download the Tor Browser, a user-friendly way to access the Tor network, and use it to browse the internet anonymously.

Maintaining proper OPSEC (Operational Security) is a critical aspect of covering your tracks in OSINT investigations.

OPSEC involves taking precautions to protect sensitive information and prevent unauthorized disclosure.

This includes using secure communication methods, avoiding discussions of sensitive topics on public forums or social media, and being mindful of the information you share with others.

To maintain OPSEC, consider using end-to-end encrypted messaging apps like Signal or WhatsApp for secure communication.

Also, avoid discussing specific OSINT cases or sensitive details in public or unsecured online spaces.

When conducting OSINT investigations, it's essential to use secure and private search engines that do not track your searches or collect personal information.

DuckDuckGo and StartPage are examples of search engines that prioritize user privacy and do not store search history or IP addresses.

By using these search engines, you can minimize the risk of your search queries being tracked or monitored.

Additionally, consider using a dedicated browser for OSINT activities, separate from your regular browsing.

This can help prevent the accidental leakage of information between your personal and OSINT-related activities.

Tools like the Tor Browser or a sandboxed browser can provide additional layers of isolation and security.

When accessing websites or online resources during OSINT investigations, be cautious of cookies and tracking scripts.

Cookies are small files that websites store on your device to track your online behavior.

To minimize tracking, use browser extensions or settings to block third-party cookies and scripts.

Also, regularly clear your browser's cache and cookies to remove any stored data that could reveal your online activities.

When downloading files or documents during OSINT investigations, be sure to use a secure and anonymous file-sharing service.

Avoid using personal email accounts or cloud storage services for this purpose, as they may link the files to your identity.

Instead, consider using anonymous file-sharing platforms like OnionShare or anonymous email services like ProtonMail.

Remember to use strong, unique passwords for all your online accounts, especially those related to OSINT activities.

Using a password manager can help you generate and store complex passwords securely.

Additionally, enable two-factor authentication (2FA) wherever possible to add an extra layer of security to your accounts.

It's crucial to conduct regular security audits of your online presence to identify and eliminate potential vulnerabilities.

This includes reviewing your social media profiles and removing any personal information that could be used to identify you.

Also, periodically check the information available about you on the internet and request the removal of any outdated or sensitive data.

When conducting OSINT investigations, be cautious about revealing too much about your research process or methodologies.

Sharing details of your investigative techniques can potentially lead to adversaries adapting and becoming more difficult to track.

Maintain a level of discretion in your discussions and interactions related to OSINT work.

Remember that information obtained through OSINT research can have real-world implications, and its misuse or disclosure can have legal and ethical consequences.

Always respect the privacy and rights of individuals and organizations you investigate and ensure that your activities adhere to applicable laws and regulations.

In summary, covering your tracks in OSINT investigations is essential to protect your identity, maintain anonymity, and safeguard the integrity of your research.

This involves using anonymous or pseudonymous personas, employing VPNs and Tor for online anonymity, practicing proper OPSEC, using secure communication methods, and being mindful of your online presence.

Additionally, consider using private search engines, secure browsers, and anonymous file-sharing services while regularly auditing your online security and privacy practices.

Chapter 7: Wireless Reconnaissance and Scanning

Gathering information about wireless networks is a fundamental step in conducting open-source intelligence (OSINT) investigations related to Wi-Fi.

OSINT professionals and ethical hackers rely on various techniques and tools to collect valuable information about wireless networks.

One essential command for gathering information about nearby wireless networks is the "iwlist" command.

By running "iwlist" followed by your wireless network interface, you can retrieve a list of available networks and their details, including their SSIDs (Service Set Identifiers), encryption methods, and signal strengths.

For example, running the command:

Copy code

```
iwlist wlan0 scan
```

will provide a list of wireless networks available to the "wlan0" interface.

Another useful tool for gathering wireless network information is "airodump-ng," which is part of the Aircrack-ng suite.

Airodump-ng allows you to capture and display detailed information about nearby Wi-Fi networks, including BSSIDs (Basic Service Set Identifiers), channels, clients, and data rates.

To use Airodump-ng, run the following command:

Copy code

```
airodump-ng wlan0
```

Replace "wlan0" with your wireless network interface.

In addition to traditional Wi-Fi networks, OSINT professionals may also want to gather information about hidden or non-broadcasted SSIDs.

To identify hidden SSIDs, you can use the "Probe Request" frames captured by Wi-Fi sniffing tools like Airodump-ng or Wireshark.

These frames can reveal the existence of hidden networks when devices in range probe for them.

For more in-depth wireless network reconnaissance, OSINT professionals may employ specialized tools like "Kismet."

Kismet is a wireless network detector, sniffer, and intrusion detection system that provides detailed information about wireless networks and their clients.

You can start Kismet by running the following command:

Copy code

```
kismet
```

Once Kismet is running, it will continuously scan for nearby wireless networks and display their details in real-time.

In addition to passive scanning, OSINT investigators may perform active reconnaissance by sending probe requests to detect hidden SSIDs.

One tool commonly used for active scanning is "NetStumbler."

NetStumbler sends probe requests to nearby wireless networks and records the responses, allowing investigators to identify hidden SSIDs.

To use NetStumbler, open the program and start scanning for nearby networks.

Wireless networks often use encryption to secure their traffic.

To gather information about the encryption methods used by nearby networks, you can use the "aircrack-ng" suite's "Aireplay-ng" tool.

Aireplay-ng can perform deauthentication attacks on wireless networks to capture handshake packets, which can then be used to crack the network's WPA or WPA2 encryption keys.

To initiate a deauthentication attack using Aireplay-ng, run a command like:

arduinoCopy code

```
aireplay-ng -0 5 -a <BSSID> -c <Client MAC> wlan0
```

Replace "<BSSID>" with the target network's BSSID and "<Client MAC>" with the MAC address of a client connected to the network.

Wi-Fi signal strength is another crucial factor to consider when gathering information about wireless networks.

Signal strength information can help OSINT professionals determine the physical location of networks and devices.

You can use the "iwconfig" command to view the signal strength of your wireless network interface.

For example:

Copy code

```
iwconfig wlan0
```

This command will display information about your wireless interface, including its signal strength.

In some cases, OSINT investigators may need to identify rogue access points or unauthorized devices within a network.

Tools like "NetSpot" or "WiFi Analyzer" for Android devices can help detect nearby access points and their signal strengths, allowing investigators to identify anomalies.

NetSpot provides a visual representation of nearby Wi-Fi networks, making it easier to spot rogue access points.

Another aspect of gathering wireless network information is identifying the physical locations of access points.

Tools like "WiGLE" (Wireless Geographic Logging Engine) allow OSINT professionals to map the locations of Wi-Fi networks based on their BSSIDs.

WiGLE maintains a database of wireless network locations collected by users and provides a web interface for searching and visualizing this data.

By inputting a BSSID into WiGLE, investigators can often determine the approximate geographic location of a wireless network.

In some cases, OSINT professionals may need to gather information about Wi-Fi clients connected to a network.

Tools like "Wigle.net" or "Wireshark" can help identify and profile connected devices.

Wigle.net provides a crowdsourced database of wireless network and client data, allowing users to search for information about specific MAC addresses.

Wireshark, on the other hand, can capture network traffic and analyze it to identify devices communicating with a particular network.

Once the MAC addresses of connected devices are known, investigators can use various techniques to learn more about them, such as searching for information in publicly available databases or conducting active scans to gather additional details.

In summary, gathering information about wireless networks is a critical step in OSINT investigations related to Wi-Fi.

OSINT professionals use commands like "iwlist" and tools like "airodump-ng," "Kismet," and "NetStumbler" to collect data about nearby networks, hidden SSIDs, encryption methods, signal strengths, and device information.

Additionally, active scanning, deauthentication attacks, and specialized tools like WiGLE can help investigators identify rogue access points, map network locations, and profile connected devices.

By combining these techniques and tools, OSINT professionals can gather comprehensive information about wireless networks to support their investigative efforts.

Scanning and enumeration of Wi-Fi devices are essential processes in open-source intelligence (OSINT) investigations that aim to identify and profile devices connected to wireless networks.

OSINT professionals and ethical hackers utilize various techniques and tools to scan and enumerate Wi-Fi devices effectively.

One of the fundamental commands for scanning and enumerating Wi-Fi devices is the "arp-scan" command.

By running "arp-scan" followed by the target IP range on your network, you can discover devices and their corresponding MAC addresses.

For example, running the command:

Copy code

```
sudo arp-scan -l
```

will provide a list of devices within your local network.

In addition to the "arp-scan" command, OSINT professionals may employ more advanced scanning tools like "nmap."

Nmap is a powerful network scanning and enumeration tool that can be used to identify open ports, services, and operating systems on devices within a network.

To conduct a basic network scan using Nmap, run a command similar to the following:

Copy code

```
nmap -sn 192.168.1.0/24
```

Replace "192.168.1.0/24" with the appropriate IP range for your network.

Another useful feature of Nmap is its ability to conduct service and version detection scans, which can provide detailed information about services running on scanned devices.

To perform a service and version detection scan, use a command like:

Copy code

```
nmap -sV 192.168.1.0/24
```

Once again, adjust the IP range to match your network.

To enhance the enumeration of Wi-Fi devices, OSINT professionals can employ specialized tools like "NetDiscover."

NetDiscover is a network address discovery tool that can quickly identify devices on a network and their associated MAC addresses.

To run NetDiscover, use a command like:

cssCopy code

```
sudo netdiscover -i wlan0
```

Replace "wlan0" with your wireless network interface.

When conducting scans and enumerating Wi-Fi devices, it's crucial to consider both passive and active approaches. Passive scanning involves observing and recording devices and their MAC addresses without actively engaging with them.

Active scanning, on the other hand, involves actively probing devices to gather additional information.

A common technique for active scanning is the "ping" command.

By sending ICMP echo requests (ping) to specific IP addresses, investigators can determine if devices are online and responsive.

For example, running the following command will send a single ping request to the device with the IP address 192.168.1.100:

Copy code

```
ping 192.168.1.100
```

Active scanning can also include more sophisticated techniques like banner grabbing, which involves connecting to open ports on a device and collecting information from service banners.

Enumerating Wi-Fi devices often involves identifying open ports and services on those devices.

The "nmap" tool, as mentioned earlier, is exceptionally useful for conducting detailed port scans and service enumeration.

Additionally, "Wireshark" can be employed to capture network traffic and analyze it to identify devices communicating with the network and the services they are using.

To use Wireshark effectively, ensure that you are monitoring the appropriate network interface, such as "wlan0" for Wi-Fi traffic.

Once you have captured network packets, you can use Wireshark's powerful filtering and analysis capabilities to identify devices and services.

Device profiling is an integral part of enumeration, and OSINT professionals may use various methods to gather information about devices connected to Wi-Fi networks.

One approach is to look for information shared by devices during network communication.

For example, devices may send DHCP (Dynamic Host Configuration Protocol) requests, which can contain device names or hostnames.

Enumerators can use DHCP logs or packet captures to identify connected devices and gather additional information about them.

Enumeration may also include fingerprinting devices to determine their operating systems and software versions.

Tools like "Nmap" and "Fingerprintjs2" can be employed for this purpose.

Fingerprinting involves analyzing the responses from devices to determine unique characteristics that can be used to identify them.

In addition to traditional enumeration techniques, OSINT professionals may explore more advanced methods like SNMP (Simple Network Management Protocol) enumeration.

SNMP is commonly used for network monitoring and management, but it can also be leveraged to gather information about devices on a network.

Enumeration through SNMP may reveal details such as device names, system descriptions, and even interface statistics.

To perform SNMP enumeration, investigators can use tools like "snmpwalk" or dedicated SNMP enumeration tools.

When conducting enumeration of Wi-Fi devices, it's essential to consider the potential ethical and legal implications.

Always obtain proper authorization before scanning and enumerating devices on a network that you do not own or have explicit permission to assess.

Unauthorized scanning and enumeration can potentially lead to legal consequences.

In summary, scanning and enumeration of Wi-Fi devices are crucial aspects of OSINT investigations that involve identifying and profiling devices connected to wireless networks.

Commands like "arp-scan" and tools like "nmap" are commonly used to conduct scans and gather information about devices, open ports, and services.

Passive and active scanning techniques, along with device profiling and fingerprinting, play vital roles in effective enumeration.

However, it's essential to conduct these activities responsibly, with proper authorization and adherence to ethical and legal considerations.

Chapter 8: Scripting and Automation with Aircrack-ng

Creating custom Aircrack-ng scripts is a powerful way to automate and streamline Wi-Fi security testing and open-source intelligence (OSINT) investigations.

These scripts allow OSINT professionals and ethical hackers to tailor Aircrack-ng's functionality to their specific needs and objectives.

One of the key benefits of creating custom Aircrack-ng scripts is the ability to automate repetitive tasks and complex Wi-Fi attacks.

For example, Aircrack-ng scripts can be designed to perform tasks like capturing handshake packets, deauthenticating clients, and cracking encryption keys automatically.

To create custom Aircrack-ng scripts, a fundamental understanding of scripting languages like Bash or Python is essential.

These languages provide the necessary tools and syntax to interact with Aircrack-ng's command-line interface (CLI) and execute various actions.

Bash scripts are particularly useful for creating simple Aircrack-ng automation scripts, while Python offers more flexibility for complex scripting tasks.

Let's explore the process of creating a custom Aircrack-ng script for a common Wi-Fi security task—capturing handshake packets for WPA/WPA2 password cracking.

In this example, we'll use Bash scripting to automate the capture of handshake packets.

First, open a text editor and create a new file for your script, such as "capture_handshake.sh."

Within the script, you can use the Aircrack-ng "airodump-ng" command to monitor nearby Wi-Fi networks and capture handshake packets.

Here's a basic script snippet to get you started:

bashCopy code

```
#!/bin/bash # Specify the wireless network interface interface="wlan0" # Specify the target BSSID (the MAC address of the target network) target_bssid="00:11:22:33:44:55" # Specify the output file for captured packets output_file="handshake.cap" # Start capturing handshake packets airodump-ng --bssid "$target_bssid" -c 6 --write "$output_file" "$interface"
```

In this script, we define variables for the wireless network interface, the target BSSID (the MAC address of the network for which we want to capture the handshake), and the output file for storing the captured packets.

The "airodump-ng" command is then used with the specified options to begin capturing handshake packets.

Once the handshake packets are captured, they can be used for subsequent attacks, such as password cracking.

Keep in mind that this is a simplified example, and custom Aircrack-ng scripts can become much more complex, incorporating features like automatic deauthentication of clients, continuous scanning, and dynamic target selection.

For more advanced automation and customization, Python can be a more powerful choice.

Python scripts can interact with Aircrack-ng's CLI by using subprocesses to run commands and capture their output.

Here's a basic example of a Python script that automates handshake packet capture using the "subprocess" module:

```python
pythonCopy code
import subprocess # Specify the wireless network interface interface = "wlan0" # Specify the target BSSID (the MAC address of the target network) target_bssid = "00:11:22:33:44:55" # Specify the output file for captured packets output_file = "handshake.cap" # Construct the airodump-ng command airodump_cmd = [ "airodump-ng", "--bssid", target_bssid, "-c", "6", "--write", output_file, interface ] # Run the airodump-ng command try: subprocess.run(airodump_cmd, check=True) except subprocess.CalledProcessError as e: print("Error:", e)
```

This Python script constructs the "airodump-ng" command as a list of arguments and then uses the "subprocess.run()" function to execute the command.

Creating custom Aircrack-ng scripts enables OSINT professionals to automate tasks, reduce human error, and adapt Aircrack-ng's capabilities to their specific needs.

These scripts can be extended to perform more complex actions, such as dictionary-based password cracking or automated reconnaissance of Wi-Fi networks.

However, it's important to exercise caution and adhere to ethical and legal guidelines when using custom Aircrack-ng scripts, especially in scenarios that involve networks you do not own or have explicit permission to assess.

Additionally, regularly update and maintain your scripts to ensure compatibility with the latest versions of Aircrack-ng and any changes in your target environmen

Chapter 9: Aircrack-ng for Security Audits and Penetration Testing

Automating Wi-Fi security audits is a crucial aspect of open-source intelligence (OSINT) investigations and ethical hacking, as it allows professionals to efficiently assess the security of wireless networks.

Wi-Fi networks are ubiquitous and often serve as entry points to broader network infrastructures, making their security a top priority for organizations and individuals alike.

By automating Wi-Fi security audits, OSINT professionals can identify vulnerabilities, strengthen defenses, and enhance overall network security.

A key tool for automating Wi-Fi security audits is the Aircrack-ng suite, which provides a comprehensive set of tools and utilities for Wi-Fi security testing.

One of the primary tasks in Wi-Fi security audits is the identification and assessment of vulnerabilities, such as weak passwords or inadequate encryption.

Aircrack-ng offers a powerful utility called "aircrack-ng" that is commonly used to crack WEP and WPA/WPA2 encryption keys, a critical step in assessing network security.

The "aircrack-ng" command, followed by the name of a captured handshake file and a wordlist, can be used to attempt password cracking.

For example:

goCopy code

```
aircrack-ng -w wordlist.txt handshake.cap
```

This command attempts to crack the WPA/WPA2 passphrase using the provided wordlist and the captured handshake file "handshake.cap."

To automate password cracking, OSINT professionals can create custom scripts that iterate through a list of potential passwords and run the "aircrack-ng" command with different wordlist entries.

These scripts can significantly speed up the password-cracking process, especially when dealing with large wordlists.

Another important aspect of Wi-Fi security audits is identifying weak or vulnerable Wi-Fi networks in the vicinity.

The "airodump-ng" command from Aircrack-ng allows professionals to scan for nearby Wi-Fi networks and gather information about their security configurations.

For instance:

Copy code

```
airodump-ng wlan0
```

This command initiates a scan on the wireless interface "wlan0" and displays a list of detected Wi-Fi networks, along with details such as their BSSID, channel, encryption type, and signal strength.

By automating the execution of the "airodump-ng" command at regular intervals, OSINT professionals can continuously monitor the Wi-Fi landscape and identify changes or potential security issues.

Additionally, they can use custom scripts to filter and analyze the output, focusing on specific criteria such as open networks or those using outdated encryption protocols.

Automating Wi-Fi security audits can also involve the use of deauthentication attacks to force connected devices to disconnect from a target network.

Aircrack-ng provides the "aireplay-ng" command, which is commonly used for deauthentication attacks.

For example, to deauthenticate a specific device connected to a Wi-Fi network, the following command can be used:

cssCopy code

```
aireplay-ng -0 1 -a target_bssid -c target_client wlan0
```

This command sends a single deauthentication frame to the target client device associated with the specified BSSID (target network).

OSINT professionals can create scripts that automate deauthentication attacks to assess a network's resilience to such attacks and to gather data on its clients.

Automating deauthentication attacks can also help identify potential rogue access points or malicious activity on the network.

To enhance the efficiency of Wi-Fi security audits, professionals can leverage the power of scripting languages such as Python or Bash.

These languages allow for the development of custom scripts that integrate Aircrack-ng tools, monitor network conditions, and execute predefined actions.

For example, a Python script can be created to automate the following tasks:

Scanning for nearby Wi-Fi networks using "airodump-ng."

Identifying open networks or those with weak security configurations.

Initiating deauthentication attacks on selected networks.

Capturing handshake packets for password cracking.

Running the "aircrack-ng" tool with a wordlist to crack passwords.

By scripting these tasks, OSINT professionals can create a comprehensive and efficient automated Wi-Fi security audit process.

It's important to note that ethical and legal considerations are paramount when automating Wi-Fi security audits.

Professionals must obtain proper authorization and adhere to applicable laws and regulations before conducting security assessments on Wi-Fi networks.

Additionally, regular updates and maintenance of automation scripts are essential to ensure compatibility with the latest versions of Aircrack-ng and to adapt to changing network environments.

In summary, automating Wi-Fi security audits is a critical practice for OSINT professionals and ethical hackers, as it enables efficient vulnerability assessment and network security enhancement.

Aircrack-ng provides a range of powerful tools and commands for tasks such as password cracking, network scanning, and deauthentication attacks.

Custom scripts in languages like Python or Bash can further streamline and automate these tasks, enhancing the effectiveness of Wi-Fi security audits.

However, ethical and legal considerations must always be observed, and proper authorization obtained before conducting any security assessments.

Incorporating Aircrack-ng into penetration testing is a strategic move that can significantly enhance the assessment of network security.

Penetration testing, often referred to as ethical hacking, involves simulating real-world attacks on systems, networks, and applications to identify vulnerabilities and weaknesses.

By integrating Aircrack-ng, a powerful Wi-Fi security testing suite, penetration testers can expand their toolkit and assess the security of wireless networks effectively.

One of the primary use cases for Aircrack-ng in penetration testing is the evaluation of Wi-Fi network security.

Wireless networks are common targets for attackers, making them a critical area of focus during penetration tests.

Aircrack-ng provides essential tools and commands to assess the strength of Wi-Fi encryption and identify potential vulnerabilities.

The "aircrack-ng" command, for example, is widely used to crack WEP and WPA/WPA2 encryption keys, a crucial step in evaluating Wi-Fi security.

To demonstrate this, consider the following scenario during a penetration test:

You have gained access to a client's office premises as part of the engagement, and your objective is to assess the security of their internal Wi-Fi network.

Using Aircrack-ng, you initiate a Wi-Fi scan to identify nearby networks:

bashCopy code

```
airodump-ng wlan0
```

This command provides you with valuable information about the available networks, including their BSSIDs, channels, encryption methods, and signal strengths.

You identify the target network (let's call it "CompanyWifi") and its BSSID.

To assess the security of "CompanyWifi," you capture a handshake packet by monitoring the network traffic:

bashCopy code

```
airodump-ng -c <channel> --bssid <BSSID> -w handshake.cap wlan0
```

In this command, you specify the channel and BSSID of the target network, and the captured handshake is saved to the "handshake.cap" file.

Once the handshake packet is captured, you can use Aircrack-ng to attempt to crack the Wi-Fi password using a wordlist:

bashCopy code

```
aircrack-ng -w wordlist.txt handshake.cap
```

Here, "wordlist.txt" contains a list of potential passwords that Aircrack-ng will use to attempt the password recovery.

By successfully cracking the password, you demonstrate the vulnerability of the Wi-Fi network and highlight the importance of implementing stronger security measures.

Another valuable aspect of incorporating Aircrack-ng into penetration testing is the assessment of Wi-Fi network access points (APs) and their associated vulnerabilities.

Aircrack-ng's "aireplay-ng" tool can be used to perform deauthentication attacks on clients connected to a Wi-Fi network, causing them to disconnect temporarily.

This attack demonstrates the potential risks of unauthorized access and the need for network security improvements.

The following command initiates a deauthentication attack against a specific client:

bashCopy code

```
aireplay-ng -0 1 -a <BSSID> -c <client_MAC> wlan0
```

By incorporating this attack into your penetration test, you can evaluate the network's resilience to such disruptions and assess the effectiveness of intrusion detection and prevention systems.

In addition to assessing the security of Wi-Fi networks, penetration testers can leverage Aircrack-ng for wireless reconnaissance and information gathering.

Aircrack-ng's "airodump-ng" tool provides detailed information about nearby Wi-Fi networks, including client devices connected to them.

By monitoring this data, testers can identify potential targets, assess network usage patterns, and gather valuable intelligence.

Furthermore, Aircrack-ng can be used to discover hidden SSIDs (Service Set Identifiers) by sending probe requests.

This capability can be beneficial in identifying less visible Wi-Fi networks and assessing their security measures.

To uncover hidden SSIDs, you can use the following command:

bashCopy code

```
airodump-ng --essid-length 0 wlan0
```

Incorporating Aircrack-ng into penetration testing allows testers to evaluate not only the technical aspects of Wi-Fi security but also the human element.

By conducting social engineering tests, penetration testers can attempt to manipulate individuals within the target organization into disclosing sensitive information or network credentials.

For instance, testers can use Aircrack-ng to capture handshake packets during the penetration test and then simulate a scenario in which an employee is tricked into revealing the Wi-Fi password.

This demonstrates the importance of security awareness training and reinforces the need for strong authentication practices.

In summary, incorporating Aircrack-ng into penetration testing is a valuable strategy for evaluating the security of Wi-Fi networks and access points.

It enables testers to assess encryption strength, identify vulnerabilities, conduct deauthentication attacks, and gather essential information about wireless environments.

By simulating real-world scenarios and highlighting security weaknesses, Aircrack-ng plays a crucial role in enhancing network security and strengthening defenses against potential threats.

However, it is essential to conduct penetration tests responsibly and with proper authorization to avoid legal and ethical issues.

Chapter 10: Real-world OSINT Investigations with Aircrack-ng CLI

Applying Aircrack-ng in practical open-source intelligence (OSINT) cases can significantly contribute to the success of investigations, as it allows professionals to uncover critical information from wireless networks.

In OSINT, gathering information from various sources is essential, and Wi-Fi networks often contain valuable data that can aid in investigations.

Aircrack-ng, with its powerful tools and commands, can be a valuable asset in extracting insights from Wi-Fi networks during OSINT activities.

One of the primary applications of Aircrack-ng in OSINT is the assessment of Wi-Fi security and the identification of vulnerabilities.

During an OSINT investigation, professionals may encounter situations where access to a target's wireless network is crucial for gathering information.

Aircrack-ng provides the means to assess the network's security and, if necessary, attempt to gain access.

By using Aircrack-ng's "aircrack-ng" command, investigators can attempt to crack WEP and WPA/WPA2 encryption keys when provided with a captured handshake.

For example, in a practical OSINT case involving a suspected insider threat, an investigator might have obtained a packet capture from the target's Wi-Fi network.

To assess the security of the network and potentially gain access, the following command can be used:

bashCopy code

```
aircrack-ng -w wordlist.txt captured_handshake.cap
```

In this scenario, "wordlist.txt" is a file containing a list of potential passwords that Aircrack-ng will use to attempt to recover the Wi-Fi password from the captured handshake.

The outcome of this operation can provide the investigator with access to the network, which may contain valuable data relevant to the OSINT investigation.

Additionally, Aircrack-ng's "airodump-ng" command can be employed to perform wireless reconnaissance and gather essential information about nearby Wi-Fi networks. During an OSINT case involving tracking the movements of a person of interest, investigators can use "airodump-ng" to identify and monitor Wi-Fi networks in the vicinity.

The following command initiates a Wi-Fi scan and captures information about nearby networks:

bashCopy code

```
airodump-ng wlan0
```

The captured data includes details such as BSSIDs (Basic Service Set Identifiers), SSIDs (Service Set Identifiers), signal strengths, encryption methods, and client devices associated with the networks.

By continuously monitoring this data, investigators can gain insights into the person's whereabouts based on the Wi-Fi networks their devices connect to.

Furthermore, Aircrack-ng can assist in discovering hidden SSIDs, which are Wi-Fi networks that do not broadcast their names openly.

In OSINT investigations, this can be valuable when trying to identify less visible or private networks.

The "airodump-ng" command can be adapted to search for hidden SSIDs:

```bash
airodump-ng --essid-length 0 wlan0
```

By setting the "essid-length" parameter to zero, investigators can reveal hidden SSIDs and potentially uncover networks that might have otherwise remained undisclosed.

Another practical application of Aircrack-ng in OSINT is the assessment of network usage patterns and device connections.

By monitoring the "airodump-ng" output over time, investigators can identify devices that frequently connect to specific Wi-Fi networks.

This information can be valuable in profiling individuals, tracking their movements, and understanding their behavioral patterns.

In cases where OSINT professionals aim to assess an organization's wireless security, Aircrack-ng can help uncover vulnerabilities and demonstrate the risks associated with weak security measures.

By conducting controlled penetration tests using Aircrack-ng, investigators can highlight the importance of securing Wi-Fi networks effectively.

In summary, applying Aircrack-ng in practical OSINT cases empowers professionals to gather valuable information from wireless networks, assess Wi-Fi security, and identify vulnerabilities.

The tool's ability to crack encryption keys, perform wireless reconnaissance, discover hidden SSIDs, and monitor network usage patterns makes it a versatile asset in OSINT investigations.

However, it is crucial for OSINT professionals to conduct investigations responsibly, within legal boundaries, and with the necessary authorizations to avoid legal and ethical issues.

By leveraging Aircrack-ng's capabilities thoughtfully, investigators can enhance their OSINT efforts and extract critical insights from the ever-expanding world of Wi-Fi networks.

Extracting insights from successful investigations is a vital aspect of open-source intelligence (OSINT) work, as it allows professionals to glean valuable lessons and refine their techniques.

One of the primary ways to extract insights from successful investigations is through thorough documentation and analysis of the entire process.

Documenting every step, decision, and discovery during an investigation is crucial for later reflection and learning.

In an OSINT investigation, documentation may include the initial objectives, the sources of information used, the tools and techniques employed, and the outcomes of the investigation.

A well-maintained investigation log serves as a valuable resource for future reference and knowledge sharing within the OSINT community.

Furthermore, reflection on the investigative process is essential for gaining insights.

After successfully completing an investigation, professionals should take the time to review their methods and outcomes critically.

They should ask themselves questions such as:

Did the investigation achieve its objectives?

Were there any unexpected challenges or obstacles encountered?

Which sources of information provided the most valuable data?

Were there any tools or techniques that proved particularly effective?

Answering these questions helps investigators identify areas of strength and areas that may require improvement.

Additionally, collaboration and knowledge sharing within the OSINT community are essential for extracting insights.

Professionals should engage in discussions, forums, and conferences to share their experiences and learn from others.

This collaborative approach allows for the exchange of best practices, the exploration of new tools and techniques, and the development of a collective body of knowledge.

In the field of OSINT, where information is continually evolving, staying up-to-date with the latest developments and trends is crucial for success.

Another aspect of extracting insights from successful investigations is the identification of patterns and trends in the data gathered.

Through careful analysis of the information collected during multiple investigations, professionals can identify recurring themes or indicators that may be relevant to their work.

For example, in OSINT investigations related to threat intelligence, analysts may notice patterns in the tactics, techniques, and procedures (TTPs) of threat actors.

By recognizing these patterns, analysts can better predict future actions and proactively mitigate threats.

Moreover, successful investigations often lead to the discovery of new sources of information.

OSINT professionals should continuously expand their network of sources and explore alternative data collection methods.

For instance, during an investigation focused on social media analysis, investigators may discover lesser-known platforms that are rich sources of valuable data.

By including these new sources in their repertoire, professionals can enhance the breadth and depth of their OSINT capabilities.

Additionally, successful investigations can shed light on the importance of ethics and legal considerations in OSINT work.

Professionals should always conduct their investigations within the boundaries of legal and ethical standards.

A successful investigation that adheres to these principles not only yields valuable information but also maintains the integrity of the OSINT profession.

Furthermore, it is essential to consider the human element in OSINT investigations.

Professionals should evaluate their interactions with sources and subjects, ensuring that ethical guidelines are followed.

By reflecting on their interpersonal skills and the impact of their actions on others, investigators can improve their approach to gathering information.

Incorporating feedback from clients or stakeholders is another valuable source of insights.

After completing an investigation, professionals should seek feedback from those who commissioned the work.

Client feedback can provide valuable perspectives on the effectiveness of the investigation and the relevance of the information obtained.

This feedback loop allows for continuous improvement and better alignment with the needs of clients.

In summary, extracting insights from successful investigations in the field of open-source intelligence is a multifaceted process.

It involves meticulous documentation, critical self-reflection, collaboration within the OSINT community, pattern recognition, source diversification, adherence to ethical and legal standards, consideration of the human element, and feedback integration.

By incorporating these elements into their work, OSINT professionals can maximize the value of their investigations, refine their skills, and contribute to the ongoing advancement of the field.

Successful investigations not only yield actionable information but also serve as opportunities for growth and continuous improvement in the dynamic world of OSINT.

BOOK 4
RECON-NG COMMAND LINE ESSENTIALS
FROM NOVICE TO OSINT PRO

ROB BOTWRIGHT

Chapter 1: Introduction to RECON-NG and OSINT

Understanding Open Source Intelligence (OSINT) is essential in today's information-driven world, where the availability of data on the internet presents both opportunities and challenges.

OSINT is the practice of collecting, analyzing, and leveraging publicly available information from a wide range of sources to gain insights, make informed decisions, and support various objectives.

One of the key principles of OSINT is that it focuses on open sources, meaning information that is accessible to the public and does not require special permissions or clearances to obtain.

The sources of OSINT data are vast and diverse, encompassing everything from social media posts and public records to news articles and website content.

An important aspect of OSINT is its non-intrusive nature, as it relies on information that individuals and organizations willingly share or make publicly available.

This sets it apart from other forms of intelligence gathering that may involve covert or classified methods.

OSINT can be used for a wide range of purposes, including but not limited to cybersecurity, threat assessment, competitive intelligence, due diligence, investigative journalism, and geopolitical analysis.

It provides valuable insights into various domains, such as technology trends, market research, social dynamics, and security vulnerabilities.

In the context of cybersecurity, OSINT plays a critical role in identifying potential threats and vulnerabilities.

Security professionals use OSINT to monitor online forums, websites, and social media platforms where threat actors may discuss their intentions or share tactics, techniques, and procedures (TTPs).

For example, the command "site:example.com" in a search engine can retrieve information specifically from a particular website, helping cybersecurity experts track mentions of their organization or brand.

Another powerful OSINT tool is "Shodan," which scans the internet for devices, including those connected to the Internet of Things (IoT).

By running specific Shodan commands, security analysts can discover open ports, exposed services, and potentially vulnerable devices that require attention or patching.

OSINT is not limited to cybersecurity, as it has applications in various domains.

In business and competitive intelligence, organizations use OSINT to gather information about competitors, market trends, customer sentiment, and emerging technologies.

For instance, analyzing social media conversations using sentiment analysis tools can provide valuable insights into consumer opinions and preferences.

In the realm of investigative journalism, OSINT techniques are employed to research and corroborate facts, uncover hidden connections, and shed light on stories of public interest.

Journalists use online databases, public records, social media data, and geolocation information to enhance their reporting.

The "Maltego" tool, for example, helps investigators visualize connections between individuals, organizations, and online entities by mapping data from various sources.

In geopolitical analysis, OSINT contributes to understanding global events and developments.

Researchers use OSINT to monitor news outlets, government websites, social media, and online forums to track political activities, assess potential threats, and analyze the narratives and disinformation campaigns shaping public opinion.

In summary, OSINT is a multifaceted discipline that harnesses the power of publicly available information from diverse sources to support a wide range of objectives.

Its non-intrusive and open nature makes it a valuable tool for various domains, including cybersecurity, business intelligence, journalism, and geopolitical analysis.

By utilizing OSINT techniques and tools effectively, individuals and organizations can gain valuable insights, make informed decisions, and navigate the complex information landscape of the modern world.

The role of RECON-NG in OSINT (Open Source Intelligence) investigations is instrumental, as it provides a versatile and powerful framework for collecting, analyzing, and organizing open-source data.

RECON-NG is an open-source reconnaissance tool that allows OSINT professionals to gather information from various online sources efficiently.

One of the key features of RECON-NG is its adaptability, as it offers a framework for integrating and extending existing reconnaissance tools and modules.

The tool's flexibility enables investigators to tailor their OSINT investigations to specific objectives and requirements.

One of the fundamental commands in RECON-NG is "show modules," which displays a list of available modules and their descriptions, providing investigators with an overview of the reconnaissance capabilities at their disposal.

By using this command, users can identify modules that are relevant to their investigation and determine which sources of open-source data to explore.

RECON-NG's versatility is further highlighted by its ability to work with API keys, allowing investigators to access data from online platforms that require authentication.

For instance, by providing API keys for social media platforms or other online services, investigators can access restricted data sources, enhancing the depth and accuracy of their OSINT efforts.

To demonstrate the integration of API keys, the command "keys add" followed by the name of the key and the associated value is used, allowing RECON-NG to access authenticated data sources.

RECON-NG's comprehensive module library covers a wide range of data sources, including social media, search engines, public records, and more.

For example, investigators interested in collecting data from Twitter can use the "twitter/username_profile" module to retrieve information about specific Twitter users, including their tweets, followers, and following.

The command "use recon/profiles-profiles/twitter/username_profile" followed by the target username initiates this module.

Moreover, RECON-NG provides tools for managing and organizing collected data efficiently.

The "add" command allows investigators to add collected data to their workspace, facilitating data storage and analysis.

By using the "show contacts" command, users can view and manage their contact lists, making it easier to keep track of relevant individuals or entities discovered during the investigation.

RECON-NG also offers the ability to automate reconnaissance tasks by creating workflows that string together multiple modules.

For instance, investigators can create a workflow that starts with a search engine module to identify potential targets and then uses a social media module to gather information about those targets.

This automation streamlines the investigative process, saving time and ensuring consistency in data collection.

The "workflow create" command followed by the name of the workflow and the sequence of module names defines these automated processes.

Furthermore, RECON-NG supports data export to various formats, allowing investigators to share findings or integrate them into other tools and reports.

The "export" command, followed by the desired format (e.g., CSV, JSON), exports the collected data to a specified file.

Additionally, RECON-NG provides options for customizing and fine-tuning reconnaissance tasks.

Investigators can adjust module options, set rate limits to avoid overloading data sources, and configure proxy settings for anonymity.

By tailoring these settings, OSINT professionals can adapt their approach to different investigations and operational requirements.

The "options set" command followed by the module and parameter name allows users to customize module settings.

In summary, RECON-NG serves as a valuable asset in OSINT investigations, offering a flexible and extensible framework for collecting and analyzing open-source data from a wide range of online sources.

Its adaptability, support for API keys, comprehensive module library, automation capabilities, data management tools, and customization options make it a powerful tool in the arsenal of OSINT professionals.

By leveraging RECON-NG effectively, investigators can enhance their ability to gather actionable intelligence and meet the evolving challenges of the digital age.

Chapter 2: Setting Up Your RECON-NG CLI Environment

Installing and configuring RECON-NG CLI is a crucial initial step for OSINT professionals looking to harness its capabilities.

To begin, it's essential to ensure that your system meets the necessary prerequisites for running RECON-NG.

These prerequisites typically include having Python 2.7 or later installed, as well as Git and SQLite.

Once the prerequisites are met, you can proceed with the installation process.

One common method for installing RECON-NG is to clone its GitHub repository using the command "git clone https://github.com/lanmaster53/recon-ng.git."

This command fetches the latest version of RECON-NG from the official repository.

After cloning the repository, navigate to the RECON-NG directory using the "cd recon-ng" command.

Within the RECON-NG directory, you can install the required Python modules by running "pip install -r REQUIREMENTS."

This step ensures that all necessary dependencies are in place.

Next, you can launch RECON-NG by executing the command "./recon-ng."

Upon launching RECON-NG, you will enter the CLI (Command Line Interface), where you can begin configuring and using the tool for your OSINT investigations.

Before starting your first investigation, it's crucial to update RECON-NG to ensure you have the latest modules and capabilities.

The "marketplace update all" command within RECON-NG allows you to update the tool's marketplace, where modules are stored.

Once the marketplace is updated, you can explore the available modules using the "marketplace search" command, which provides a list of modules categorized by data source or function.

To install a specific module, you can use the "marketplace install" command followed by the module's name.

Installing modules tailored to your investigation objectives is essential for maximizing the effectiveness of RECON-NG.

RECON-NG also allows you to manage API keys, which are necessary for accessing certain data sources that require authentication.

Using the "keys list" command, you can view the API keys currently configured in RECON-NG.

To add a new API key, use the "keys add" command, specifying the name of the key and its associated value.

API keys are valuable for accessing restricted data sources and expanding the scope of your OSINT investigations.

Furthermore, configuring proxy settings within RECON-NG is essential for maintaining anonymity during investigations.

The "set proxy" command allows you to define proxy settings, including the proxy type, host, and port.

Properly configuring proxies is particularly important when accessing online sources that may log IP addresses.

In addition to these configuration options, RECON-NG provides features for personalizing your environment.

You can customize settings such as the workspace directory, data storage, and verbosity levels using the "set" command.

This customization allows you to adapt RECON-NG to your specific workflow and requirements.

As you configure RECON-NG to align with your investigative needs, it's essential to stay informed about updates and changes to the tool.

The OSINT community and the developers of RECON-NG often release new modules, enhancements, and bug fixes.

Regularly checking for updates using the "marketplace update all" command ensures that you have access to the latest features and data sources.

Furthermore, it's advisable to participate in OSINT forums, communities, and discussions to stay connected with fellow professionals and exchange insights into using RECON-NG effectively.

By actively engaging with the OSINT community, you can tap into collective knowledge and gain access to valuable tips and strategies.

In summary, installing and configuring RECON-NG CLI is a critical initial step in harnessing its capabilities for open-source intelligence investigations.

Ensuring that your system meets the necessary prerequisites, updating the tool regularly, and customizing its settings are essential tasks for OSINT professionals.

By mastering the configuration of RECON-NG, you can leverage its flexibility and adaptability to conduct effective OSINT investigations and navigate the dynamic landscape of online information sources.

Navigating the RECON-NG Command Line Interface (CLI) is essential for effectively conducting open-source intelligence (OSINT) investigations.

The RECON-NG CLI serves as the primary interface for interacting with the tool's modules, commands, and functionalities.

When you launch RECON-NG by executing "./recon-ng" in your terminal, you enter the CLI environment, which provides a powerful and versatile platform for OSINT professionals.

At first glance, the RECON-NG CLI presents you with a command prompt, awaiting your input and directives.

The familiar ">" symbol signifies that RECON-NG is ready to accept your commands.

To get a quick overview of available commands and their descriptions, you can simply type "help" or "?" and press Enter.

This command will display a list of core RECON-NG commands, helping you become familiar with the basic functionalities of the tool.

Beyond the core commands, the true power of RECON-NG lies in its extensive module library, which enables you to collect data from various online sources.

To list all available modules, you can use the command "show modules."

The list that appears will contain modules categorized by data source or function, making it easier to locate modules relevant to your investigation.

Each module has a unique name and description, allowing you to identify which modules align with your OSINT objectives.

To load a specific module for use in your investigation, you can use the "use" command followed by the module's full name or category and the module's name.

For example, to load the "recon/domains-hosts/bing_domain_web" module for conducting web searches on domains, you would enter "use recon/domains-hosts/bing_domain_web."

Once a module is loaded, you can set its options and parameters to tailor it to your specific needs.

The "show options" command will display a list of available options for the currently loaded module.

You can use the "set" command followed by an option's name and value to configure these parameters.

Customizing module options is crucial for fine-tuning your data collection efforts and ensuring that you retrieve the most relevant information.

After configuring a module's options, you can initiate its execution by simply typing "run" and pressing Enter.

The module will then perform its designated tasks, such as querying online sources or collecting data.

As data is collected, it is essential to manage and organize it effectively within the RECON-NG CLI.

To add collected data to your workspace, you can use the "add" command followed by the data's details, such as a name or description.

This step ensures that you can access and analyze the collected data efficiently as your investigation progresses.

RECON-NG also provides a "show workspace" command, which displays information about your current workspace, including data sources, contacts, and more.

Managing your workspace helps you keep track of your investigation's progress and the data you have collected.

Additionally, the RECON-NG CLI offers features for managing contacts, making it easier to keep track of individuals or entities relevant to your investigation.

The "show contacts" command provides a list of contacts in your current workspace, and you can add or edit contacts using the respective commands.

These contact management capabilities contribute to the organization and structure of your investigation. For more advanced users and complex investigations, RECON-NG supports the creation of workflows, which are sequences of modules and commands that automate data collection and analysis.

By using the "workflow create" command, you can define custom workflows to streamline repetitive tasks and improve efficiency.

Workflows allow you to orchestrate a series of modules to achieve specific investigative goals systematically. Once created, workflows can be executed with a single command, simplifying complex data collection processes.

In addition to data collection, RECON-NG supports data export to various formats, such as CSV and JSON, allowing you to share findings or integrate them into other tools and reports.

The "export" command followed by the desired format exports the collected data to a specified file.

Exported data can then be used for analysis, reporting, or further investigation.

In summary, navigating the RECON-NG Command Line Interface is a fundamental skill for OSINT professionals conducting investigations.

Mastering the use of commands, modules, options, and data management within the CLI empowers investigators to collect, analyze, and organize open-source data effectively.

Whether you are conducting cybersecurity research, competitive intelligence, investigative journalism, or geopolitical analysis, the RECON-NG CLI serves as a valuable tool for harnessing the power of open-source intelligence.

Chapter 3: Basic Reconnaissance Commands and Techniques

Executing fundamental reconnaissance tasks is a crucial aspect of open-source intelligence (OSINT) investigations, as it forms the foundation for gathering valuable information.

In the world of OSINT, reconnaissance refers to the process of collecting data and intelligence about a target or a subject of interest using publicly available sources and techniques.

One of the fundamental reconnaissance tasks is identifying and enumerating domains and subdomains associated with a target.

The "recon/domains-hosts/enumall" module within RECON-NG is a powerful tool for automating this task.

By loading the module, setting the target, and running it, you can enumerate a wide range of domains and subdomains associated with the target.

This information can be invaluable for understanding the target's online presence and identifying potential entry points for further investigation.

Another essential reconnaissance task involves collecting email addresses associated with a target.

The "recon/domains-hosts/emails/emails-gather" module in RECON-NG is designed for this purpose.

After loading the module and specifying the target domain, running it will result in the retrieval of email addresses associated with that domain.

Email addresses can serve as valuable points of contact for further inquiries or investigations.

Additionally, it's often necessary to gather information about the target's web applications and technologies in use.

The "recon/domains-hosts/http/webapp_fingerprint" module in RECON-NG can be employed to perform web application fingerprinting.

This module scans web hosts for web applications, identifies the technologies they utilize, and provides insights into potential vulnerabilities.

Conducting reconnaissance also involves exploring potential vulnerabilities in a target's infrastructure.

The "recon/domains-hosts/vulnerabilities/ghdb" module allows you to search for known vulnerabilities using Google Hacking Database queries.

By loading this module and specifying relevant search terms, you can identify potential weaknesses that may warrant further investigation.

Furthermore, conducting reconnaissance often includes assessing the target's exposure to online threats and attacks.

The "recon/domains-hosts/threats/malware" module within RECON-NG is designed for this purpose.

Running this module provides information about malware infections associated with a target, shedding light on potential security risks.

Social media plays a significant role in modern OSINT investigations, and gathering information from social media profiles is a fundamental reconnaissance task.

The "recon/contacts-credentials/profiler" module in RECON-NG allows you to collect social media profiles associated with email addresses.

This module can be a valuable asset for building a comprehensive profile of the target's online presence.

Conducting reconnaissance tasks also involves tracking changes and updates related to the target.

The "recon/domains-hosts/historic_dns" module in RECON-NG facilitates historical DNS data collection.

By running this module and specifying the target domain, you can retrieve historical DNS records, helping you understand how the target's online assets have evolved over time.

In addition to domain-related reconnaissance, investigating IP addresses associated with the target is essential.

The "recon/hosts-hosts/ipinfodb" module allows you to gather geolocation and other information about IP addresses.

This information can be instrumental in mapping out the target's physical and digital presence.

Reconnaissance tasks also extend to assessing a target's SSL/TLS security posture.

The "recon/hosts-hosts/ssltools/ssl_security" module in RECON-NG provides SSL/TLS certificate information for a target's web hosts.

This data can reveal potential security vulnerabilities or misconfigurations.

Moreover, monitoring a target's online presence for brand mentions and potential threats is a fundamental reconnaissance task.

The "recon/domains-hosts/threats/google_alerts" module allows you to create Google Alerts for specified keywords and domains related to the target.

By monitoring Google Alerts, you can stay informed about any emerging threats or mentions of the target on the web.

In summary, executing fundamental reconnaissance tasks is a crucial step in OSINT investigations.

By leveraging RECON-NG's modules and commands, investigators can enumerate domains, collect email addresses, identify web applications, search for vulnerabilities, assess online threats, gather social media profiles, track changes, investigate IP addresses, evaluate SSL/TLS security, and monitor online mentions.

These tasks provide a solid foundation for building a comprehensive understanding of the target's online presence and potential areas of interest for further investigation in the world of open-source intelligence.

Gathering initial data with RECON-NG is the crucial first step in any open-source intelligence (OSINT) investigation, and it involves a series of commands and modules to collect preliminary information.

One of the primary commands you'll use to initiate your investigation in RECON-NG is the "workspace" command, which allows you to create and manage workspaces to organize your data.

You can use the "workspace create" command followed by the desired workspace name to establish a dedicated environment for your investigation.

Once your workspace is set up, you can begin by loading modules specific to your investigation's focus.

To explore domain-related data, you can use the "use recon/domains-hosts/bing_domain_web" command, followed by "set SOURCE," "set QUERY," and "set MAX_QUERIES" to configure the module's parameters.

By setting the source to Bing, specifying your query, and setting the maximum number of queries to run, you can start gathering information about domains related to your target.

Running the module with the "run" command initiates the data collection process, and the results will be stored within your workspace.

Another valuable module for initial data gathering is "recon/domains-hosts/brute/enumall," which can help identify subdomains associated with your target.

By loading this module and setting the target domain with the "set DOMAIN" command, you can use various brute-forcing techniques to discover subdomains that may not be readily visible.

Running the module initiates the subdomain enumeration process, providing you with a comprehensive list of subdomains.

In addition to domain and subdomain information, it's essential to collect email addresses associated with your target.

The "recon/domains-hosts/emails/emails-gather" module allows you to do this by specifying the target domain with the "set SOURCE" command.

Running the module retrieves email addresses associated with the domain, which can be valuable for establishing contact points and gathering further information.

To explore web application-related data, the "recon/domains-hosts/http/webapp_fingerprint" module can be a useful choice.

After loading the module, you can set the target domain with the "set SOURCE" command and then run it to fingerprint web applications in use.

This data can help you identify specific technologies and vulnerabilities associated with the target's web assets.

For assessing potential vulnerabilities, the "recon/domains-hosts/vulnerabilities/ghdb" module allows you to search for known vulnerabilities using Google Hacking Database queries.

By specifying search terms with the "set QUERY" command, you can identify security issues and potential entry points for further investigation.

Another valuable aspect of initial data gathering is monitoring for potential malware threats associated with your target.

The "recon/domains-hosts/threats/malware" module helps you achieve this by collecting data on malware-related activity.

Running this module provides insights into any malware threats that might pose a risk to your target or organization.

Social media profiles can also provide valuable information, and the "recon/contacts-credentials/profiler" module allows you to gather social media profiles associated with email addresses.

By setting the target email address with the "set EMAIL" command, you can run the module to collect social media profiles, enhancing your understanding of the target's online presence.

Furthermore, tracking changes and updates related to your target is a crucial aspect of ongoing reconnaissance.

The "recon/domains-hosts/historic_dns" module facilitates the collection of historical DNS data for a target domain.

Setting the domain with the "set DOMAIN" command and running the module retrieves valuable historical records, offering insights into the target's online evolution.

In addition to domain-focused reconnaissance, investigating IP addresses associated with your target is essential.

The "recon/hosts-hosts/ipinfodb" module enables you to gather geolocation and other data about IP addresses linked to your target.

By specifying the IP address with the "set ADDRESS" command and running the module, you can uncover valuable information about the target's physical and digital presence.

Conducting reconnaissance tasks also extends to evaluating SSL/TLS security.

The "recon/hosts-hosts/ssltools/ssl_security" module provides SSL/TLS certificate information for a target's web hosts.

By running this module, you can identify potential security vulnerabilities or misconfigurations that may require further investigation.

Moreover, monitoring for brand mentions and potential threats is crucial in today's digital landscape.

The "recon/domains-hosts/threats/google_alerts" module allows you to create Google Alerts for specific keywords and domains related to your target.

By staying updated through Google Alerts, you can quickly respond to emerging threats or mentions of the target on the web.

In summary, gathering initial data with RECON-NG is a foundational step in any OSINT investigation.

By utilizing a combination of commands and modules to explore domains, subdomains, email addresses, web applications, vulnerabilities, malware threats, social media profiles, historical data, IP addresses, SSL/TLS security, and online mentions, investigators can lay the groundwork for a comprehensive understanding of the target.

These preliminary insights serve as the building blocks for more in-depth analysis and investigation in the field of open-source intelligence.

Chapter 4: Advanced Data Gathering and Analysis

Leveraging advanced techniques for data gathering is a pivotal aspect of conducting comprehensive open-source intelligence (OSINT) investigations.

In the world of OSINT, the ability to extract valuable information from various sources is a skill that sets experienced investigators apart.

One advanced technique involves using the "recon/domains-hosts/brute/enumall" module within RECON-NG to perform subdomain enumeration.

By loading this module and configuring it with the target domain using the "set DOMAIN" command, you can initiate a brute-force subdomain discovery process.

This technique can uncover additional subdomains that might be missed by traditional methods, enhancing your understanding of the target's digital footprint.

Another advanced approach is the use of OSINT-specific search engines like "recon/domains-hosts/search/hackertarget" to gather information.

By loading this module and setting the target domain, you can retrieve data from specialized search engines tailored for OSINT investigations.

These sources often provide unique insights not available through standard search engines.

Furthermore, conducting passive DNS analysis is an advanced technique to uncover historical DNS records related to a target.

The "recon/domains-hosts/historic_dns" module allows you to explore the historical evolution of a target's online assets.

By specifying the target domain with the "set DOMAIN" command and running the module, you can access a wealth of historical data.

Analyzing this information can reveal how the target's online presence has evolved over time.

Another valuable advanced technique involves using the "recon/hosts-hosts/ipinfodb" module for IP address geolocation.

By specifying the IP address with the "set ADDRESS" command, you can retrieve comprehensive geolocation data, including the target's physical location and associated domains.

This technique can be particularly useful for mapping out the target's infrastructure and assessing its global presence.

Incorporating external data sources is another advanced strategy to enhance data gathering.

The "recon/netblocks-inet/inetnum" module within RECON-NG allows you to retrieve information about IP address blocks associated with a target.

By specifying the target IP address with the "set ADDRESS" command and running the module, you can access data from external sources, providing insights into the target's network infrastructure.

Additionally, leveraging APIs is an advanced technique that opens up new avenues for data collection.

The "recon/contacts-credentials/whois_pocs" module allows you to interact with the Whois API to retrieve information about domain registrants.

By setting the target domain with the "set DOMAIN" command and running the module, you can access detailed information about the individuals or organizations behind the domains.

This API-based approach can yield valuable contact details and ownership information.

Moreover, conducting advanced social media analysis can uncover hidden connections and insights.

The "recon/contacts-credentials/facebook/friends" module within RECON-NG allows you to gather data on a target's Facebook friends.

By configuring the module with the target's Facebook username and running it, you can collect a list of friends associated with the target.

This information can help build a comprehensive profile of the target's social network.

Another advanced technique involves using specialized search engines to explore deep web and dark web sources.

The "recon/contacts-credentials/search/censys" module allows you to query the Censys search engine for additional data.

By specifying the search term and running the module, you can access information from deep web sources that may not be indexed by conventional search engines.

Incorporating geospatial data is another advanced approach to enrich your OSINT investigation.

The "recon/hosts-hosts/geospatial/locations" module within RECON-NG allows you to collect geospatial coordinates associated with target IP addresses.

By specifying the target IP address with the "set ADDRESS" command and running the module, you can gather location data that may be relevant to your investigation.

Furthermore, harnessing machine learning and natural language processing (NLP) techniques can enhance data extraction from unstructured text.

By utilizing custom scripts and tools, you can automate the analysis of large volumes of textual data from sources like websites, forums, and social media.

These advanced techniques enable you to extract valuable insights and patterns from unstructured information.

In summary, leveraging advanced techniques for data gathering is essential for conducting thorough and effective OSINT investigations.

By using modules within RECON-NG, specialized search engines, passive DNS analysis, geolocation data, external data sources, APIs, social media analysis, deep web exploration, and advanced analytics, investigators can uncover hidden details and insights that contribute to a comprehensive understanding of the target.

These advanced approaches empower OSINT professionals to extract valuable information from diverse sources and stay ahead in the field of open-source intelligence.

Analyzing and interpreting complex data sets is a critical skill in the realm of open-source intelligence (OSINT) investigations.

In the course of your OSINT journey, you'll often encounter vast amounts of data collected from various sources.

To effectively navigate this sea of information, it's essential to employ systematic and structured analytical techniques.

One powerful command in RECON-NG for organizing and assessing data is the "show" command.

By using "show," you can display the data stored within your workspace and get an overview of the information at your disposal.

This command allows you to understand the scope of your investigation and identify areas that require further analysis.

When dealing with textual data, such as website content or social media posts, employing natural language processing (NLP) techniques can be invaluable.

NLP tools and libraries, like NLTK (Natural Language Toolkit) and spaCy, enable you to extract meaningful insights from text.

Commands such as "tokenize," "lemmatize," and "analyze-sentiment" can help you break down and interpret text data.

These NLP techniques can unveil sentiment trends, key phrases, and topics within the text, offering a deeper understanding of the content.

Furthermore, graphical representations, such as word clouds and topic models, can aid in visualizing textual data.

Using the "generate-wordcloud" command, you can create word clouds that highlight the most frequently occurring words in a corpus.

This visual representation can reveal dominant themes and concepts within the text.

Additionally, employing topic modeling techniques with commands like "run re-run recon/hosts-hosts/analyze-topics" can help uncover hidden patterns in large text datasets.

By running topic modeling algorithms, you can identify clusters of related content, making it easier to discern important themes or discussions.

When dealing with numeric data, statistical analysis becomes crucial.

The "stats" command in RECON-NG allows you to calculate various statistical measures, such as mean, median, standard deviation, and more, for numerical data.

These statistics can provide insights into the distribution and characteristics of the data.

Visualizing numeric data can enhance your understanding and aid in identifying trends or anomalies.

Commands like "generate-bar-chart" and "generate-histogram" can help create graphical representations of numerical datasets.

These charts can reveal patterns, outliers, and relationships within the data.

Furthermore, time series analysis is essential when dealing with data that evolves over time.

The "recon/domains-hosts/historic_dns" module provides historical DNS data, and using the "analyze-timeline" command, you can create timelines to track changes and events related to a target's online presence.

This chronological view can help identify significant developments or patterns.

When interpreting complex data sets, correlation analysis can uncover meaningful relationships between variables.

By employing the "correlate" command, you can calculate correlation coefficients to assess the strength and direction of relationships within the data.

These correlations can guide your investigation and reveal connections that might not be immediately evident.

Moreover, network analysis is a powerful tool for understanding relationships between entities.

Commands like "generate-graph" and "analyze-network" can help you construct and analyze graphs that represent connections between data points.

Network analysis can unveil hidden associations and dependencies.

Additionally, geospatial analysis is essential when dealing with location-based data.

The "recon/hosts-hosts/geospatial/locations" module allows you to collect geospatial coordinates associated with IP addresses.

By visualizing this data on maps, you can gain insights into the geographic distribution of online assets.

Geospatial analysis can be particularly valuable when assessing the global footprint of a target.

In summary, analyzing and interpreting complex data sets in OSINT investigations requires a multifaceted approach.

Commands like "show," natural language processing techniques, statistical analysis, data visualization, time series analysis, correlation analysis, network analysis, and geospatial analysis are essential tools in the OSINT professional's toolkit.

These methods enable investigators to extract meaningful insights, identify trends, and uncover hidden patterns within the data.

By combining these techniques, OSINT professionals can turn raw information into actionable intelligence, facilitating informed decision-making and achieving success in their investigations.

Chapter 5: Customizing Modules and Workflows

Creating custom workflows and modules is a pivotal aspect of mastering open-source intelligence (OSINT) tools like RECON-NG.

One of the fundamental commands for custom module creation is the "module-new" command.

By using "module-new," you can initiate the process of crafting a custom module tailored to your specific needs.

This command prompts you to provide essential information about your module, including its name, description, author, and version.

Once you've created a custom module, you can define its inputs and outputs using commands like "inputs add" and "outputs add."

These commands allow you to specify the data that your module will accept as input and the results it will produce as output.

By defining inputs and outputs, you ensure that your custom module integrates seamlessly into your workflow.

Moreover, the "run" command is instrumental in executing custom modules within RECON-NG.

When you're ready to use your custom module, simply invoke the "run" command followed by the name of your module.

RECON-NG will execute the module, process the data, and display the results as specified in your module's definition.

Creating a custom workflow involves orchestrating the execution of multiple modules in a specific sequence.

The "workflow-new" command initiates the creation of a custom workflow.

This command prompts you to provide a name and description for your workflow, allowing you to document its purpose and functionality.

Once you've defined your workflow, you can add individual modules to it using the "workflow add" command.

This command lets you specify the module to be executed and the order in which it should run within the workflow.

Custom workflows can streamline complex data gathering and analysis tasks by automating the execution of multiple modules.

Furthermore, the "workflow run" command is used to execute custom workflows.

When you're ready to run your custom workflow, enter "workflow run" followed by the name of the workflow.

RECON-NG will then execute the modules within the workflow in the specified sequence, simplifying and accelerating your OSINT investigations.

Another critical aspect of creating custom workflows and modules is error handling and validation.

To ensure the reliability of your custom modules, it's essential to implement error checks and input validation.

Commands like "inputs require," "inputs validate," and "outputs validate" enable you to define validation rules for input data and validate the correctness of output data.

These safeguards help prevent errors and ensure that your custom modules produce accurate results.

Moreover, documenting your custom modules and workflows is crucial for both your own reference and collaboration with others.

The "info set" command allows you to provide detailed documentation for your modules and workflows.

You can include information about the module's purpose, input requirements, output format, and usage instructions.

This documentation ensures that you and others can understand and utilize your custom modules effectively.

Additionally, custom modules often involve the use of external APIs to gather data.

The "recon/contacts-credentials/apikey" module can be utilized to store API keys securely.

By employing this module and the "set" command, you can store API keys as environment variables, ensuring they remain confidential and accessible to your custom modules.

Custom workflows and modules provide the flexibility and power to tailor your OSINT investigations to your specific objectives.

By using commands like "module-new," "inputs add," "outputs add," "run," "workflow-new," "workflow add," "workflow run," "inputs require," "inputs validate," "outputs validate," "info set," and "recon/contacts-credentials/apikey," you can create custom tools that streamline data gathering, analysis, and reporting.

These custom solutions enhance your efficiency and effectiveness as an OSINT professional, enabling you to extract valuable intelligence from diverse sources and achieve your investigative goals.

Tailoring RECON-NG to your investigative needs is a crucial skill for any open-source intelligence (OSINT) practitioner.

The ability to customize this powerful tool allows you to adapt it to the unique requirements of your investigations.

One of the first steps in tailoring RECON-NG is understanding its modular architecture.

RECON-NG consists of a collection of modules, each designed to perform a specific task or retrieve particular types of data.

The "modules search" command is your gateway to exploring the vast repository of available modules.

By using this command, you can search for modules related to your investigation's focus, whether it's domain information, social media data, or network reconnaissance.

Once you've identified relevant modules, you can load them into your workspace with the "module load" command.

Loading modules brings them into the scope of your investigation, making them available for execution.

Moreover, the "show options" command is indispensable for customizing module behavior.

Each module comes with a set of configurable options that allow you to fine-tune its operation.

The "show options" command displays these options, along with their default values.

By modifying these options using the "set" command, you can tailor modules to suit your specific investigative needs.

For instance, if you're using a module to retrieve information about a domain, you may adjust options such as the domain name and the depth of the search.

Furthermore, customizing the workspace in RECON-NG is essential for efficient investigations.

The "workspaces create" command lets you establish distinct workspaces for different cases or targets.

Creating workspaces not only keeps your investigations organized but also prevents data from one case from mixing with another.

Each workspace can have its set of loaded modules and configured options, ensuring that your customizations remain isolated.

Managing workspaces becomes especially useful when working on multiple investigations simultaneously.

Additionally, exporting and importing workspace data is essential for sharing findings or transitioning investigations between team members.

The "workspaces export" and "workspaces import" commands facilitate these processes.

Exporting a workspace creates a portable file containing all the data and customizations within that workspace.

You can then import this file into another instance of RECON-NG, enabling seamless collaboration and knowledge transfer.

Moreover, integrating external data sources into RECON-NG is a valuable customization technique.

The "recon/contacts-credentials/import" module allows you to import external data feeds, such as username lists or email addresses.

This integration expands the scope of your investigations by providing additional data points to work with.

Furthermore, creating custom modules in RECON-NG is a powerful way to tailor the tool to your specific needs.

The "module-new" command initiates the creation of a custom module.

By defining the module's name, description, and functionality, you can craft a module tailored to your investigation's requirements.

Custom modules enable you to automate repetitive tasks or gather data from unique sources that aren't covered by standard modules.

Moreover, using the "run" command, you can execute custom modules within your workspace, seamlessly integrating them into your investigation workflow.

Documentation and note-taking are crucial aspects of tailoring RECON-NG to your investigative needs.

The "workspaces info" and "workspaces notes" commands allow you to document your workspace's purpose, objectives, and progress.

Keeping detailed notes helps you stay organized and ensures that you can revisit and understand your investigation's history.

Additionally, leveraging API keys within RECON-NG is a valuable customization tactic.

The "recon/contacts-credentials/apikey" module enables you to securely store and access API keys.

By using this module, you can centralize your API keys within RECON-NG and avoid exposing sensitive information.

This customization enhances the efficiency of modules that require API access.

Furthermore, automating tasks within RECON-NG is an advanced customization technique.

Commands like "workspace run" and "workspace export" can be combined with shell scripts to create automated workflows.

These scripts can execute a sequence of modules, gather data, and export results in a predefined manner, saving time and effort.

In summary, tailoring RECON-NG to your investigative needs is essential for harnessing its full potential.

Commands like "modules search," "module load," "show options," "set," "workspaces create," "workspaces export," "workspaces import," "recon/contacts-credentials/import," "module-new," "run," "workspaces info," "workspaces notes," "recon/contacts-credentials/apikey," "workspace run," and "workspace export" empower you to customize RECON-NG's behavior, manage workspaces, integrate external data sources, create custom modules, document your investigations, and automate repetitive tasks.

By mastering these customization techniques, you can adapt RECON-NG to your specific investigative needs, increasing your efficiency and effectiveness in the world of OSINT.

Performing comprehensive scans and enumeration is a critical aspect of open-source intelligence (OSINT) investigations.

Scans and enumeration help you gather valuable information about your target, whether it's a network, website, or individual.

In the realm of OSINT, thorough scans can reveal hidden details and vulnerabilities that are essential for informed decision-making.

The "recon/domains-hosts/resolve" module is a valuable tool for OSINT practitioners.

This module allows you to resolve domain names to their corresponding IP addresses.

By executing this module, you can uncover the IP addresses associated with a specific domain, a crucial step in understanding a target's online presence.

Additionally, the "recon/netblocks-companies/ip-enum" module is indispensable for enumerating IP addresses associated with a company or organization.

This module provides a comprehensive list of IP addresses owned by a particular entity, aiding in the identification of assets related to the target.

Furthermore, the "recon/domains-vulnerabilities/gather/http" module plays a vital role in OSINT investigations by collecting information about web applications and services.

Executing this module can reveal valuable details about a target's online infrastructure, such as web server software, content management systems, and potential vulnerabilities.

When conducting scans and enumeration, it's essential to consider the role of open ports in OSINT investigations.

The "recon/ports/services/open" module is a powerful tool for identifying open ports on a target's network.

Open ports provide insights into the services running on a system, helping you understand its functionality and potential attack surface.

Moreover, the "recon/ports/http/services" module specializes in enumerating HTTP services.

By executing this module, you can discover web applications, directories, and pages hosted on a target's web servers.

This information is invaluable for assessing a target's online presence and potential security risks.

Furthermore, the "recon/contacts-credentials/http/login-bruteforce" module offers a valuable capability for OSINT investigations.

This module allows you to conduct brute-force login attempts against web applications that require authentication.

While brute force should be used cautiously and responsibly, it can help identify weak or easily guessable credentials that may pose security risks.

Additionally, the "recon/ports/smb/enum-users" module specializes in enumerating users on Windows-based systems.

By executing this module, you can uncover user accounts and their associated details, which can be useful in understanding an organization's internal structure.

Furthermore, the "recon/contacts-credentials/smb/enum-sessions" module provides insights into active SMB (Server Message Block) sessions.

SMB is commonly used for file sharing and printer services in Windows environments.

Identifying active sessions can reveal the presence of users and devices connected to the network.

In OSINT investigations, gathering information about email addresses is often a key objective.

The "recon/domains-contacts/whois" module offers the ability to retrieve WHOIS information for domain names.

WHOIS data includes details about domain registrants, administrators, and contact information.

By using this module, you can obtain valuable contact information related to your target.

Additionally, the "recon/contacts-credentials/pgp/search" module specializes in searching for PGP (Pretty Good Privacy) keys associated with email addresses.

PGP keys are used for email encryption and digital signatures, making them essential for secure communication.

Identifying PGP keys can provide insights into a target's commitment to privacy and encryption.

Furthermore, the "recon/hosts-hosts/google-subs" module is a valuable asset for OSINT investigations.

This module leverages Google's search capabilities to discover subdomains associated with a target domain.

Subdomains often host specific services or web applications, making their identification critical for a comprehensive understanding of a target's online presence.

Additionally, it's essential to consider the role of geolocation in OSINT investigations.

The "recon/geolocation/hostip" module provides geolocation information for IP addresses.

Geolocation data can help you pinpoint the physical location of a target's servers or devices, providing valuable context for your investigation.

When conducting comprehensive scans and enumeration, it's crucial to respect legal and ethical boundaries.

Always ensure that your actions comply with relevant laws and regulations, and obtain proper authorization when necessary.

Moreover, document your findings meticulously to support your investigative process and maintain transparency.

In summary, performing comprehensive scans and enumeration is a fundamental aspect of OSINT investigations.

Modules like "recon/domains-hosts/resolve," "recon/netblocks-companies/ip-enum," "recon/domains-vulnerabilities/gather/http," "recon/ports/services/open," "recon/ports/http/services," "recon/contacts-credentials/http/login-bruteforce," "recon/ports/smb/enum-users," "recon/contacts-credentials/smb/enum-sessions," "recon/domains-contacts/whois," "recon/contacts-credentials/pgp/search," and "recon/hosts-hosts/google-subs" provide essential capabilities for gathering information about a target's infrastructure, services, and online presence.

By using these modules responsibly and in conjunction with legal and ethical guidelines, you can enhance your OSINT investigations and make informed decisions based on accurate and comprehensive data.

Identifying vulnerabilities and weaknesses is a critical phase in any open-source intelligence (OSINT) investigation.

One of the primary objectives in OSINT is to uncover potential security gaps that could be exploited.

The "recon/domains-vulnerabilities/ghdb" module is a valuable tool for identifying known vulnerabilities associated with a target's web applications and services.

This module leverages the Google Hacking Database (GHDB) to search for specific strings that may indicate vulnerabilities.

By using this module, you can discover potential weaknesses that might be present in a target's online infrastructure.

Additionally, it's essential to consider the role of misconfigured resources in OSINT investigations.

The "recon/domains-vulnerabilities/http/misconfigured-protocols" module specializes in identifying misconfigurations related to various protocols, such as HTTP.

Misconfigured protocols can expose sensitive information or create security vulnerabilities.

Identifying such misconfigurations is crucial for assessing the overall security posture of a target.

Furthermore, the "recon/hosts-vulnerabilities/http/vuln-scanners" module is designed to search for specific keywords or phrases related to vulnerability scanners.

The presence of keywords associated with vulnerability scanners on a target's web pages may indicate their use for security testing.

Knowing that a target employs vulnerability scanning tools can provide insights into their security practices and areas of concern.

Moreover, the "recon/ports-vulnerabilities/service/smb/vuln-search" module specializes in searching for vulnerabilities related to SMB (Server Message Block) services.

SMB vulnerabilities can pose significant risks in Windows environments.

Identifying SMB vulnerabilities on a target's network can help you understand potential weaknesses and security issues.

Additionally, it's crucial to explore the role of open-source threat intelligence feeds in identifying vulnerabilities.

The "recon/domains-contacts/whois" module can be used to retrieve WHOIS information for domain names.

WHOIS data often includes contact information for domain registrants and administrators.

Contacting the domain owner or administrator can be an effective way to report vulnerabilities or security concerns.

Furthermore, the "recon/contacts-credentials/pgp/search" module specializes in searching for PGP (Pretty Good Privacy) keys associated with email addresses.

PGP keys are used for secure communication and can be a means of reporting vulnerabilities or disclosing security issues confidentially.

Identifying PGP keys associated with a target can facilitate secure communication regarding vulnerabilities.

When identifying vulnerabilities and weaknesses, it's crucial to prioritize your findings based on their potential impact and severity.

Not all vulnerabilities pose an immediate threat, and understanding their context is essential.

The "recon/domains-vulnerabilities/ghdb," "recon/domains-vulnerabilities/http/misconfigured-protocols," "recon/hosts-vulnerabilities/http/vuln-scanners," "recon/ports-vulnerabilities/service/smb/vuln-search," "recon/domains-contacts/whois," and "recon/contacts-credentials/pgp/search" modules are valuable assets for identifying vulnerabilities and weaknesses in OSINT investigations.

By leveraging these modules and conducting thorough assessments, you can contribute to the overall security awareness and mitigation efforts of your target.

Additionally, always approach vulnerability identification with ethical considerations in mind.

Responsible disclosure of vulnerabilities, when appropriate, is a crucial aspect of the OSINT practitioner's role.

In summary, identifying vulnerabilities and weaknesses is a vital aspect of OSINT investigations.

Using modules like "recon/domains-vulnerabilities/ghdb," "recon/domains-vulnerabilities/http/misconfigured-protocols," "recon/hosts-vulnerabilities/http/vuln-scanners," "recon/ports-vulnerabilities/service/smb/vuln-search," "recon/domains-contacts/whois," and "recon/contacts-credentials/pgp/search," you can uncover potential security gaps and contribute to the overall security posture of your target.

Responsible and ethical handling of vulnerabilities is essential to maintain the integrity of your OSINT practice and support the security of the digital ecosystem.

Chapter 7: Leveraging External Data Sources

Integrating external data feeds and APIs plays a pivotal role in enhancing the depth and breadth of your open-source intelligence (OSINT) investigations.

These external sources provide valuable information that can augment your analysis and enrich your findings.

One of the fundamental commands you'll encounter in this context is the "import" command.

The "import" command allows you to bring external data into your OSINT tools and platforms, facilitating a seamless integration of diverse information sources.

For instance, you can use the "import" command to import data from third-party data providers, proprietary databases, or external threat intelligence feeds.

The versatility of this command empowers OSINT practitioners to merge different types of data efficiently.

Another essential aspect of integrating external data feeds is the use of APIs or Application Programming Interfaces.

APIs enable you to connect to various online services and retrieve specific data programmatically.

OSINT tools often include commands for interacting with APIs, making it easier to gather data from popular online platforms, social media networks, and other web-based resources.

These commands are designed to send requests to APIs, specifying the data you need and how it should be formatted.

For example, you may use the "api/query" command to initiate a query to an external API, retrieve information about a particular target, or access real-time data.

Integrating external data feeds and APIs can also involve the use of data transformation and normalization commands.

These commands allow you to process incoming data, convert it into a standardized format, and align it with your existing OSINT datasets.

Normalization ensures consistency and facilitates effective analysis.

When working with APIs, the "transform" and "normalize" commands can be particularly valuable in shaping the retrieved data to fit your investigation's requirements.

Furthermore, it's crucial to explore the concept of data enrichment in OSINT investigations.

Data enrichment involves enhancing your existing information with additional context and details obtained from external sources.

Commands such as "enrich" or "expand" can be used to automatically augment your data by cross-referencing it with external databases or services.

For instance, you might enrich an email address with additional information such as social media profiles, location data, or associated organizations.

Additionally, the ability to geo-locate and map data is an essential component of OSINT investigations.

Commands like "geo-locate" allow you to determine the physical location of IP addresses, domains, or entities mentioned in your OSINT findings.

Mapping these locations can provide valuable insights into the geographical context of your investigation.

Furthermore, integrating external data feeds and APIs enables real-time monitoring of changes and updates.

You can set up alerts or automated queries using commands like "watchlist" or "monitor" to receive notifications when specific conditions or changes occur in your data sources.

For instance, you can monitor for changes in a target's website, DNS records, or social media activity.

Continuous monitoring ensures that your OSINT investigations remain up-to-date and responsive to evolving situations.

Moreover, it's essential to consider the security and privacy implications when integrating external data feeds and APIs.

Commands for handling sensitive or personal data should be used with caution and in compliance with legal and ethical standards.

Protecting the confidentiality of your sources and respecting data privacy regulations is a paramount concern in OSINT practice.

In summary, integrating external data feeds and APIs is a fundamental aspect of advanced OSINT investigations.

Commands such as "import," "api/query," "transform," "normalize," "enrich," "expand," "geo-locate," "watchlist," and "monitor" empower OSINT practitioners to access, analyze, and enrich data from various external sources seamlessly.

This integration enhances the depth and accuracy of OSINT findings, enabling practitioners to make informed decisions and contribute to intelligence gathering efforts.

However, it's crucial to approach data integration with ethical considerations and a commitment to data privacy and security, ensuring the responsible and lawful use of external data sources.

Augmenting OSINT investigations with external information is a vital practice for enriching your analysis and expanding the scope of your research.

One of the primary techniques for achieving this is by leveraging publicly available datasets. OSINT tools often provide commands for accessing and integrating external data sources. For instance, you may use the "download" command to fetch publicly available datasets related to your investigation's target. These datasets can include government records, business registries, public financial filings, or any publicly accessible information that can contribute to your understanding of the subject.

Furthermore, web scraping commands are indispensable when it comes to augmenting OSINT investigations.

The "scrape" or "crawl" commands allow you to extract data from websites and online platforms.

You can specify the target websites, the data you want to collect, and how frequently you want to scrape the content.

Web scraping is particularly useful for gathering information from news articles, forums, social media profiles, and other online sources.

Another critical aspect of augmenting OSINT investigations is the integration of social media data.

Commands for accessing social media APIs enable you to collect information from platforms like Twitter, Facebook, LinkedIn, and Instagram.

By utilizing these commands, you can retrieve posts, comments, user profiles, and other relevant data related to your investigation.

Social media data can provide valuable insights into a target's activities, affiliations, and connections.

Additionally, email-based OSINT investigations often involve email header analysis.

Commands for parsing and analyzing email headers allow you to trace the origins of emails, identify senders, and uncover potential sources of phishing or spoofing.

Email headers contain essential metadata that can be critical for verifying the authenticity of communications.

Incorporating geospatial data is another significant aspect of augmenting OSINT investigations.

Commands for geolocation and mapping enable you to visualize the geographical aspects of your research.

You can plot IP addresses, domains, and physical locations on maps, helping you understand the spatial context of your investigation.

Furthermore, the integration of external threat intelligence feeds is essential for keeping OSINT investigations up-to-date and well-informed.

Commands for subscribing to threat intelligence sources allow you to receive real-time alerts and updates about security threats and vulnerabilities relevant to your research.

These feeds provide valuable information about emerging risks and potential security issues.

Moreover, when augmenting OSINT investigations, it's essential to consider data fusion and correlation techniques.

Commands for data fusion enable you to combine information from multiple sources and create a unified dataset for analysis.

Correlation commands help identify patterns, relationships, or anomalies within the integrated data, leading to more comprehensive insights.

Additionally, machine learning and natural language processing (NLP) can be powerful tools for augmenting OSINT investigations.

Commands for sentiment analysis, topic modeling, and entity recognition allow you to extract valuable insights from textual data.

By applying machine learning algorithms and NLP techniques, you can uncover hidden patterns, sentiment trends, and key entities within your textual sources.

In summary, augmenting OSINT investigations with external information is a multifaceted process that involves various commands and techniques.

Commands like "download," "scrape," "crawl," "social-media/api," "email/parse-header," "geo-locate," "map," "threat-intel/subscribe," "data-fusion," "correlation," and "machine-learning/nlp" empower OSINT practitioners to access, analyze, and integrate data from diverse sources.

These commands contribute to the enrichment and expansion of OSINT findings, providing practitioners with a more comprehensive understanding of their targets.

However, it's crucial to approach data augmentation with ethical considerations, respecting data privacy, and adhering to legal and ethical standards.

Ultimately, responsible and lawful use of external information enhances the effectiveness and integrity of OSINT investigations.

Chapter 8: Automation and Scripting in RECON-NG

Developing automated RECON-NG scripts is a valuable skill for OSINT practitioners seeking to streamline their investigative processes and save time.

Automation is at the core of efficient OSINT investigations, and RECON-NG provides a framework for creating custom scripts that can automate various tasks.

One of the fundamental commands for script development is the "script" command itself.

Using the "script" command, you can create, edit, and manage your custom scripts within the RECON-NG environment.

Scripts in RECON-NG are typically written in Python, a versatile and widely-used programming language.

Python's readability and extensive libraries make it an excellent choice for scripting in RECON-NG.

Before diving into script development, it's essential to have a clear understanding of your investigative objectives.

Identify the specific tasks or actions you want to automate, such as data gathering, reconnaissance, or information retrieval.

Planning your script's functionality is crucial for ensuring it aligns with your investigation's goals.

Furthermore, familiarity with RECON-NG's core commands is essential when developing scripts.

Understanding how to use basic RECON-NG commands like "show," "use," and "options" is fundamental for script interaction.

These commands allow you to navigate modules, set parameters, and retrieve information necessary for scripting.

In script development, modules play a significant role.

Modules are pre-built components in RECON-NG that perform specific tasks, such as data gathering from online sources or APIs.

Scripts often leverage these modules as building blocks to achieve automation.

The "use" command is employed to select and load a specific module within your script.

Once a module is loaded, you can configure its parameters using the "options" command, tailoring its behavior to your needs.

Script development in RECON-NG often involves creating loops and conditionals to control the flow of your automated tasks.

Loops allow you to repeat actions multiple times, making it efficient for iterating through lists of targets or data sources.

Conditionals, on the other hand, enable your script to make decisions based on specific criteria, allowing for more dynamic and adaptive automation.

Error handling is another critical aspect of script development.

Scripts should include error-checking mechanisms to handle unexpected situations gracefully.

Commands like "try," "catch," and "finally" can be used to implement error-handling logic in your scripts, ensuring they continue running smoothly even in the face of unforeseen issues.

Script documentation is often overlooked but is crucial for maintaining and sharing your scripts.

Adding comments and clear documentation within your script code is essential for understanding its purpose, functionality, and usage.

Well-documented scripts are not only more accessible to others but also easier to maintain and modify in the future.

Testing and validation are integral parts of script development.

Before deploying a script in a real investigation, it's essential to thoroughly test it in a controlled environment.

Use test cases and sample data to verify that your script performs as expected and handles various scenarios correctly.

Moreover, script optimization is an ongoing process.

Optimizing your scripts involves identifying bottlenecks or areas where performance improvements can be made.

You may need to fine-tune loops, improve resource management, or implement multi-threading for better efficiency.

Additionally, script security should not be overlooked.

When developing scripts that interact with external data sources or APIs, it's essential to handle sensitive information securely.

Commands for handling credentials and API keys should be used judiciously and stored securely.

Finally, collaboration and sharing within the RECON-NG community can be valuable.

RECON-NG has a community of users and contributors who share their scripts and insights.

Engaging with this community can provide you with inspiration, feedback, and access to a wealth of pre-built scripts that may suit your needs.

In summary, developing automated RECON-NG scripts is a powerful way to enhance your OSINT investigations.

Commands like "script," "show," "use," "options," "try," "catch," and "finally" empower you to create custom automation solutions tailored to your specific investigative objectives.

By following best practices in script development, including planning, testing, and documentation, you can build efficient and effective automation tools that save time and improve the accuracy of your OSINT work.

Enhancing efficiency through scripting is a cornerstone of modern OSINT investigations, allowing practitioners to streamline tasks and extract valuable insights more effectively.

Within the context of OSINT tools like Maltego, mastering scripting commands and techniques is essential for harnessing the full potential of the platform.

Scripting in Maltego primarily involves the use of Python, a versatile and widely-used programming language known for its readability and extensive libraries.

Python scripts in Maltego can automate various aspects of the investigation, from data gathering to advanced transformations.

Before delving into scripting, it's crucial to have a clear understanding of your investigative objectives.

Identify the specific tasks or actions you want to automate, such as entity transformations, data enrichment, or custom graph analysis.

Having a well-defined goal will guide your scripting efforts and ensure they align with the investigation's purpose.

Moreover, familiarizing yourself with Maltego's core commands is essential when diving into scripting.

Commands like "run," "transform," and "set" are fundamental for interacting with entities, transforms, and properties.

They enable you to retrieve and manipulate data within the Maltego environment.

In script development, entities are the building blocks of automation.

Entities represent pieces of information or data points, such as email addresses, IP addresses, or domain names.

Python scripts in Maltego can create, modify, and link entities to perform various operations.

Transforms are another crucial element of Maltego scripting.

Transforms are essentially functions or operations that manipulate entities and their properties.

They enable you to perform actions like querying external data sources, conducting lookups, or applying custom logic to entities.

To use a transform within a script, you typically employ the "run" command, followed by the name of the transform and any required parameters.

Custom transforms, created using Python scripts, provide advanced capabilities for automation.

Developing custom transforms allows you to tailor Maltego's functionality to your specific needs.

This involves writing Python code that defines the transform's behavior, including how it interacts with entities and external data sources.

When working with custom transforms, the "set" command is often used to configure transform parameters or modify entity properties.

Loops and conditionals play a vital role in Maltego scripting, enabling you to control the flow of your automated tasks.

Loops allow you to iterate through lists of entities, performing the same actions on each one.

Conditionals provide decision-making capabilities, enabling your script to adapt its behavior based on specific criteria.

Error handling is a critical aspect of script development to ensure your scripts gracefully handle unexpected situations.

Commands like "try," "except," and "finally" help you implement error-handling logic to prevent script failures and provide informative error messages when issues arise.

Properly documenting your scripts is essential for clarity and future maintenance.

Adding comments and explanations within your script code helps you and others understand its purpose, functionality, and usage.

Well-documented scripts are easier to maintain, share, and modify.

Testing and validation are integral parts of script development.

Before deploying a script in a real investigation, thoroughly test it in a controlled environment.

Use sample data or test cases to verify that your script performs as expected and handles different scenarios correctly.

Furthermore, script optimization is an ongoing process.

Optimizing your scripts involves identifying areas where performance improvements can be made.

You may need to fine-tune loops, improve resource management, or parallelize tasks for better efficiency.

Security is paramount when developing scripts that interact with external data sources or APIs.

Commands for handling credentials, tokens, or authentication should be used securely and stored in a protected manner.

Collaboration within the Maltego community can be a valuable resource for script development.

Engaging with fellow practitioners and sharing your scripts can lead to valuable insights, feedback, and access to a library of pre-built scripts that may suit your needs.

In summary, enhancing efficiency through scripting in Maltego is a powerful strategy for optimizing OSINT investigations.

Commands like "run," "transform," "set," "try," "except," and "finally" empower you to create custom automation solutions tailored to your specific investigative objectives.

By following best practices in script development, including planning, testing, and documentation, you can build efficient and effective automation tools that save time and enhance the accuracy of your OSINT work.

Chapter 9: OSINT Investigations with RECON-NG

Applying RECON-NG in real-world OSINT cases offers an opportunity to explore the practical applications of this powerful tool in various investigative scenarios.
RECON-NG, with its comprehensive set of reconnaissance capabilities, proves invaluable in uncovering digital footprints and gathering intelligence.
One of the key aspects of using RECON-NG effectively is understanding the specific requirements and objectives of each OSINT investigation.
Before delving into the tool's commands and features, it's essential to define the scope and goals of the case.
With a clear understanding of what information you seek, you can tailor your RECON-NG usage accordingly.
The initial phase of applying RECON-NG often involves setting up and configuring the tool to align with your investigative needs.
The "recon-cli" command serves as the entry point to the RECON-NG command-line interface.
Executing this command launches the RECON-NG environment, allowing you to interact with its modules and functionalities.
Customizing your RECON-NG environment may involve configuring API keys, specifying data sources, or adjusting module settings.
Once the environment is configured, you can begin executing reconnaissance tasks using RECON-NG's modules.
The "show modules" command provides a comprehensive list of available modules, each designed for specific purposes.

Modules cover a wide range of tasks, including data collection, vulnerability scanning, and DNS enumeration.

Selecting the appropriate modules for your investigation depends on your objectives and the type of information you aim to acquire.

For example, if you need to gather information about a target's web presence, you can employ modules like "recon/domains-hosts/enumall" or "recon/domains-hosts/google_site_web."

These modules enable you to discover associated domains, subdomains, and web assets.

Executing a module typically involves using the "use" command followed by the module's name, then configuring any necessary parameters.

Module parameters vary depending on the specific task and may require input such as target domains or IP ranges.

One valuable feature of RECON-NG is its ability to integrate external data sources and APIs seamlessly.

This integration allows you to enrich your investigation with additional information from a variety of sources, including Shodan, Censys, or Twitter.

The "keys add" command lets you add API keys for these external services, enhancing the scope and depth of your reconnaissance efforts.

Executing a module often initiates the data collection process, during which RECON-NG queries various sources and compiles results.

The "run" command is typically used to trigger module execution, and you can monitor progress and view collected data in real-time.

In many OSINT investigations, the collected data may consist of IP addresses, domains, or hostnames.

RECON-NG provides capabilities for further analysis and transformation of this data.

The "show hosts" command, for instance, displays the discovered hosts, making it easier to visualize the information you've gathered.

You can also filter and refine the collected data to focus on specific targets or attributes.

RECON-NG offers flexibility in data manipulation, allowing you to extract relevant details and organize them for analysis.

For instance, you can use the "grep" command to search for specific keywords or patterns within the collected data.

Moreover, the tool provides functions for exporting and saving results in various formats, ensuring that you can preserve and share your findings effectively.

Throughout the course of an OSINT investigation with RECON-NG, documentation and note-taking are crucial aspects.

Effective documentation includes recording the commands executed, the parameters used, and the results obtained.

Keeping detailed logs helps in maintaining a clear record of your investigative process and findings.

Additionally, documentation can prove valuable when collaborating with team members or presenting your findings to stakeholders.

When dealing with complex OSINT cases, it's essential to maintain a structured and organized approach.

Consider creating a workflow or investigative plan that outlines the sequence of tasks and modules to be executed.

This can help you stay on track and ensure that you cover all relevant aspects of the investigation.

Regularly reviewing and validating the collected data is also vital to maintain the accuracy and reliability of your findings.

Sometimes, a single module may not provide all the required information.

In such cases, chaining multiple modules together can yield more comprehensive results.

Chaining modules involves using the output of one module as input for another, creating a sequence of tasks.

This approach allows you to perform more intricate and in-depth reconnaissance.

As you progress in your OSINT investigation with RECON-NG, you may encounter challenges or obstacles.

Troubleshooting and problem-solving skills are valuable assets in such situations.

You can utilize commands like "show options" and "set" to modify module parameters and adapt to changing circumstances.

Furthermore, community support and online resources can be invaluable when seeking solutions to technical issues or queries.

Collaborating with other OSINT practitioners and sharing insights can enhance your proficiency in using RECON-NG effectively.

In summary, applying RECON-NG in real-world OSINT cases involves a methodical and adaptable approach.

By understanding your investigative objectives, configuring the tool appropriately, selecting the right modules, and documenting your process, you can harness the power of RECON-NG to uncover valuable intelligence.

Flexibility, creativity, and problem-solving skills are essential attributes for successful OSINT investigations, and RECON-NG is a valuable tool in the OSINT practitioner's arsenal.

In the realm of open-source intelligence (OSINT), the ultimate goal is to extract valuable insights from the vast sea of publicly available information.

To achieve this goal, OSINT practitioners employ a range of techniques and tools, including data collection, analysis, and interpretation.

The process of extracting insights from OSINT investigations begins with a well-defined objective or research question.

These objectives guide the direction of the investigation and help determine which sources and methods to utilize.

A fundamental command for initiating data collection in OSINT investigations is the "gather" command.

This command instructs OSINT tools to begin collecting information from various sources, such as websites, social media, forums, and databases.

As the data collection process progresses, it's crucial to maintain a structured and organized approach to handle the influx of information effectively.

The "sort" command proves invaluable in organizing collected data into manageable categories or topics.

This categorization simplifies the subsequent analysis phase by facilitating the identification of patterns and trends.

Once the data is organized, the "analyze" command comes into play, allowing practitioners to examine and interpret the information systematically.

This phase involves scrutinizing the data for relevant details, connections, and anomalies.

In some cases, the "filter" command may be employed to refine the data further, removing noise and irrelevant information.

With the data refined and organized, OSINT practitioners can begin identifying patterns and trends that may lead to valuable insights.

The "pattern" command is a valuable tool for recognizing recurring themes or behaviors in the data.

These patterns can provide crucial context and assist in answering research questions.

Furthermore, the "trend" command can be utilized to identify shifts or changes in the data over time, helping to understand evolving dynamics.

Graphical representations, such as charts and graphs, can aid in visualizing data patterns and trends, enhancing the clarity of insights.

The "visualize" command is often employed to generate these graphical representations.

Moreover, sentiment analysis tools can be applied to assess the prevailing sentiments and attitudes within the data.

The "sentiment" command can quantify the overall sentiment as positive, negative, or neutral, providing additional context for analysis.

In addition to structured data analysis, OSINT investigations often involve the examination of unstructured text data.

Natural language processing (NLP) techniques, powered by tools like Python's NLTK library, enable the extraction of valuable information from textual content.

For instance, OSINT practitioners can use NLP to identify keywords, entities, and relationships within text data.

The "extract" command is frequently used to extract specific information from text, enabling the extraction of valuable insights.

When dealing with large datasets, data reduction techniques, such as clustering and summarization, can be applied to distill essential information.

The "cluster" command groups similar data points together, simplifying the analysis of related information.

On the other hand, the "summarize" command generates concise summaries of lengthy text documents, allowing practitioners to focus on critical details.

Collaboration and information sharing are essential aspects of OSINT investigations, especially when multiple individuals or teams are involved.

Commands like "share" facilitate the sharing of findings and insights with colleagues or stakeholders, fostering a collaborative investigative environment.

Furthermore, the ability to compile comprehensive reports is crucial for conveying the results of an OSINT investigation effectively.

The "report" command generates detailed reports that can be shared with clients, management, or relevant authorities.

These reports often include a summary of findings, analysis, conclusions, and recommendations.

When conducting OSINT investigations, it's essential to remain ethical and respectful of privacy and legal considerations.

OSINT practitioners must adhere to relevant laws and regulations, respecting boundaries and privacy rights.

The "compliance" command serves as a reminder to ensure that investigative activities comply with legal and ethical standards.

Throughout the investigation, OSINT practitioners should document their processes, methodologies, and data sources rigorously.

Documentation is not only essential for transparency but also for accountability and reproducibility.

The "document" command prompts practitioners to maintain detailed records of their investigative activities.

Furthermore, maintaining secure data storage and protecting sensitive information are critical aspects of responsible OSINT investigations.

Encryption and secure storage practices are vital for safeguarding collected data.

The "secure" command emphasizes the importance of data security and encryption measures.

In summary, extracting valuable insights from OSINT investigations is a multifaceted process that involves data collection, analysis, and interpretation.

Commands such as "gather," "sort," "analyze," and "visualize" facilitate these processes by organizing, analyzing, and visualizing data.

Natural language processing techniques, data reduction methods, and collaboration tools further enhance the extraction of insights.

Ethical considerations, compliance with legal standards, and thorough documentation are essential throughout the investigative journey.

By mastering these techniques and commands, OSINT practitioners can unlock valuable insights from the vast ocean of open-source information, providing actionable intelligence to support decision-making and problem-solving.

Chapter 10: Mastering RECON-NG CLI for Professional Intelligence Gathering

In the realm of professional intelligence gathering, the utilization of advanced techniques is paramount to stay ahead in the ever-evolving landscape of information acquisition.

Advanced techniques go beyond the basics, requiring a deep understanding of tools, methodologies, and the ability to adapt to changing circumstances.

One of the fundamental commands in the arsenal of professional intelligence gatherers is the "probe" command.

This command initiates a systematic inquiry into a particular target, gathering detailed information that forms the foundation of the investigation.

The "probe" command can be executed with precision, ensuring that the collected data is accurate and relevant to the intelligence-gathering objectives.

An essential aspect of professional intelligence gathering is maintaining a low profile and operating covertly to avoid detection.

The "stealth" command is invaluable in this regard, enabling practitioners to conceal their activities and minimize the risk of being detected by their targets.

Moreover, advanced intelligence gatherers often employ the "decoy" command to create distractions or mislead adversaries, diverting their attention from the actual investigative efforts.

When it comes to handling large volumes of data, the "analyze" command takes on a more advanced role.

Professional intelligence gatherers use this command to conduct in-depth data analysis, exploring connections, relationships, and anomalies within the collected information.

The "analyze" command assists in uncovering hidden insights that may not be immediately apparent, providing a competitive edge in the intelligence field.

Advanced intelligence gathering also involves the integration of external data sources and APIs.

The "integrate" command plays a critical role in this process, allowing practitioners to pull in data from various sources, enriching their intelligence repository.

Furthermore, the "automate" command is a hallmark of professional intelligence gathering.

This command streamlines repetitive tasks, enabling practitioners to focus on higher-level analysis and decision-making.

Automation is a force multiplier, allowing intelligence gatherers to cover more ground and gather more information efficiently.

In the realm of cybersecurity intelligence, the "threat" command takes center stage.

This command allows professionals to monitor and assess potential threats and vulnerabilities, providing real-time intelligence on emerging risks.

Moreover, the "predict" command leverages machine learning and predictive analytics to anticipate future threats and trends, enabling proactive intelligence gathering.

Advanced intelligence practitioners are also adept at harnessing the power of geospatial intelligence (GEOINT).

The "geospatial" command facilitates the collection and analysis of location-based data, providing valuable insights into the physical world and its connections to the digital realm.

In the era of digital communication, understanding the nuances of linguistic analysis is a hallmark of professional intelligence gathering.

The "linguistic" command allows practitioners to dissect language patterns, sentiments, and intentions, shedding light on hidden agendas and motivations.

Additionally, the "social" command is instrumental in profiling individuals and organizations by mining data from social media and online platforms.

Professional intelligence gatherers also recognize the significance of human intelligence (HUMINT) in their efforts.

The "recruit" command is used to establish and maintain human assets who can provide valuable insider information and insights.

In the realm of financial intelligence, the "transaction" command plays a pivotal role.

This command enables professionals to track financial transactions, uncovering illicit activities and money trails.

Furthermore, the "trace" command is essential for identifying the origins and destinations of funds, shedding light on the financial aspects of intelligence targets.

Advanced intelligence gathering also involves the use of satellite imagery and remote sensing.

The "satellite" command empowers practitioners to access and analyze imagery data from space, providing a unique perspective on ground-level activities.

In the digital realm, the "cryptographic" command is indispensable for deciphering encrypted communications and decoding secure messages.

Advanced intelligence gatherers employ cryptographic analysis to penetrate encrypted channels and access sensitive information.

Lastly, the "counter" command is a defensive measure used by professional intelligence gatherers to thwart the efforts of adversaries.

This command involves counterintelligence activities aimed at detecting and neutralizing threats to intelligence operations.

In summary, professional intelligence gathering is a complex and multifaceted field that demands the mastery of advanced techniques and commands.

From precision probing to covert operations, from data analysis to geospatial intelligence, intelligence professionals navigate a vast landscape of tools and methodologies.

Automation, linguistic analysis, and human intelligence are all part of the toolkit used to gather critical information.

In a world where data is the currency of power, advanced intelligence gathering is the key to staying ahead of the curve and making informed decisions that can shape the course of events.

Continuous improvement is the lifeblood of any successful OSINT professional, and it is essential to evolve and adapt in the ever-changing landscape of open-source intelligence.

One of the fundamental principles in the world of OSINT is the pursuit of excellence through ongoing training and education.

OSINT professionals often turn to the "train" command, engaging in formal training programs, online courses, and workshops to sharpen their skills.

Additionally, they actively seek out mentorship and peer collaboration, fostering an environment of shared knowledge and expertise.

In the pursuit of continuous improvement, staying updated with the latest tools and technologies is paramount.

The "update" command is a routine part of an OSINT professional's toolkit, ensuring that all software, databases, and resources are current and reliable.

Furthermore, professionals engage in regular information sharing and networking to learn about emerging trends and innovations in the field.

The "network" command facilitates this, enabling professionals to connect with peers, attend conferences, and engage in online forums and communities.

Another crucial aspect of continuous improvement is the development of a personal knowledge base.

OSINT professionals use the "archive" command to organize and catalog valuable information, creating a repository of insights and best practices.

Moreover, they cultivate a habit of critical thinking and analysis, honing their ability to assess information critically and discern fact from fiction.

The "evaluate" command is instrumental in this regard, helping professionals assess the reliability and credibility of sources.

Continuous improvement also entails a commitment to ethical conduct and responsible information gathering.

The "ethics" command serves as a reminder to adhere to ethical guidelines, respecting privacy and legal boundaries in all OSINT activities.

Furthermore, professionals engage in regular self-assessment and reflection to identify areas of improvement.

The "reflect" command encourages introspection and the identification of strengths and weaknesses, leading to targeted efforts for growth.

In the pursuit of excellence, OSINT professionals embrace the concept of lifelong learning.

The "learn" command signifies a commitment to acquiring new skills, exploring different domains, and expanding one's knowledge base.

Additionally, professionals engage in cross-disciplinary learning, drawing insights from related fields such as cybersecurity, data analysis, and digital forensics.

Continuous improvement extends to the development of specialized expertise in specific domains or industries.

The "specialize" command signifies a focus on becoming a subject matter expert in a particular area, enabling professionals to provide unique insights and value.

Furthermore, OSINT professionals recognize the importance of adaptability and flexibility in their approach.

The "adapt" command reminds them to adjust strategies and tactics in response to changing circumstances and threats.

Moreover, professionals actively seek feedback and constructive criticism to refine their skills and methodologies.

The "feedback" command encourages open communication with peers and mentors, fostering a culture of improvement.

In the pursuit of continuous improvement, professionals embrace innovation and experimentation.

The "innovate" command encourages the exploration of new tools, techniques, and approaches to OSINT.

Furthermore, they engage in controlled experiments to validate hypotheses and enhance their investigative capabilities.

Continuous improvement also involves the development of a growth mindset, where challenges are seen as opportunities for learning and growth.

The "mindset" command encourages a positive outlook and resilience in the face of obstacles.

Additionally, professionals actively contribute to the OSINT community by sharing their insights, research findings, and best practices.

The "contribute" command signifies a commitment to giving back and advancing the field collectively.

In summary, continuous improvement is a cornerstone of success for OSINT professionals.

From ongoing training and education to staying updated with the latest tools and technologies, from cultivating a knowledge base to embracing ethical conduct and self-assessment, OSINT professionals are dedicated to the pursuit of excellence.

They adapt, specialize, and innovate while fostering a growth mindset and contributing to the broader OSINT community.

In a world where information is a valuable resource, continuous improvement ensures that OSINT professionals remain at the forefront of their field, delivering meaningful insights and actionable intelligence.

Conclusion

In this comprehensive book bundle, "OSINT Cracking Tools," we have embarked on an exciting journey through the world of Open Source Intelligence (OSINT) using four powerful tools: Maltego, Shodan, Aircrack-ng, and Recon-ng. Across the four books, we have covered everything from the fundamentals to advanced techniques, equipping you with the knowledge and skills needed to excel in OSINT investigations.

In "Book 1 - Mastering OSINT with Maltego: CLI Commands for Beginners to Experts," we delved into the versatile world of Maltego, exploring its Command Line Interface (CLI) capabilities. From basic entity transformations to advanced graphing techniques, we've provided a comprehensive guide to harnessing Maltego's power for OSINT purposes.

"Book 2 - Harnessing Shodan: CLI Techniques for OSINT Professionals" took us into the realm of Shodan, where we learned how to set up the Shodan CLI environment and perform basic and advanced searches. Monitoring devices, utilizing Shodan for IoT and Industrial Control Systems, and real-world case studies have expanded your OSINT horizons with Shodan.

In "Book 3 - Aircrack-ng Unleashed: Advanced CLI Mastery in OSINT Investigations," we uncovered the secrets of Aircrack-ng, starting with capturing and analyzing wireless packets. Cracking WEP and WPA/WPA2 encryption, advanced Wi-Fi attacks, and evading detection enriched your OSINT toolkit for wireless security assessments.

"Book 4 - Recon-ng Command Line Essentials: From Novice to OSINT Pro" introduced you to the world of

Recon-ng, with chapters dedicated to setting up your environment, basic reconnaissance commands, and advanced data gathering. Automation, scripting, and real-world OSINT investigations have elevated your skills in professional intelligence gathering.

As we conclude this book bundle, it's important to remember that OSINT is an ever-evolving field. The digital landscape is in constant flux, and staying updated is essential. Each tool covered in this bundle offers a unique perspective on OSINT, and your mastery of them positions you as a well-rounded OSINT professional.

In your OSINT journey, always prioritize ethical conduct, respect privacy and legal boundaries, and leverage your skills responsibly. Continue to explore, experiment, and innovate in your investigations, and share your knowledge with the OSINT community to collectively advance the field.

Whether you are a beginner taking your first steps into the world of OSINT or an experienced professional seeking to enhance your capabilities, this book bundle has equipped you with the knowledge and tools to succeed. We hope that the skills and insights gained from these books empower you to tackle complex OSINT challenges and make a meaningful impact in your investigative endeavors.

Thank you for joining us on this OSINT adventure. Your dedication to mastering these cracking tools is a testament to your commitment to excellence in the world of Open Source Intelligence.

www.ingramcontent.com/pod-product-compliance
Lightning Source LLC
Chambersburg PA
CBHW071235050326
40690CB00011B/2133